Anne Kelly's evocative and nostalgic work often incorporates portraits – of friends, family, historical figures and even pets. In this fascinating book she shares her approach to textile portraiture, bringing in a wealth of different techniques including hand and machine embroidery, quilting and appliqué, to render in cloth the nuances of facial expressions and the personalities of her subjects. Subjects include:

• Selfies at Home: making the perfect self-portrait in cloth.

• Representation and Culture: how portraits have been used in textile art for cultural expression around the world.

• Stylized Imagery: going beyond the traditional portrait into abstraction.

• Place and Time: creating a sense of place with portraiture, sometimes incorporating photographs.

• Narratives: how to create a fuller story using deeply personal ephemera and related imagery.

• Pet Projects: immortalising your pets in your textile work.

Beautifully illustrated with stunning examples of her own work and that of intriguing textile artists who specialise in portraiture from around the world, this is the ideal book for embroiderers and textile artists who want to introduce this often tricky but always rewarding subject area into their work.

Textile Portraits

Textile Portraits

Anne Kelly

BATSFORD

First published in the United Kingdom in 2023 by
B. T. Batsford Ltd
43 Great Ormond Street
London
WC1N 3HZ

An imprint of B. T. Batsford Holdings Limited

ISBN 978 1 84994 753 4

A CIP catalogue record for this book is available from the
British Library.

10 9 8 7 6 5 4 3 2 1

Reproduction by Rival Colour Ltd, UK
Printed and bound by Toppan Leefung Printing International Ltd, China

This book can be ordered direct from the publisher at
www.batsfordbooks.com, or try your local bookshop

Contents

Introduction   6

Chapter 1
Selfies at Home   8

Chapter 2
Representation and Culture   28

Chapter 3
Stylized Imagery   48

Chapter 4
Place and Time   68

Chapter 5
Narratives   86

Chapter 6
Pets and Animals   106

Conclusion   120

Featured Artists and Contributors   122

For Investigation   124

Further Reading   125

Suppliers   126

Acknowledgements   127

Index   128

Page 1: Anne Kelly
Stay at Home (detail),
mixed-media textile.

Page 2: Anne Kelly,
Me and My Doll
(detail), mixed-media
textile.

Opposite: Marna
Lunt, stitched badges,
hand embroidery on
metal frame.

Below: Anne Kelly,
studio shelf.

Introduction

Portraits can add an extra layer of meaning to a composition. We notice the style of the subject – their appearance and pose – and relate it to a time and place in the rest of the composition. Portraiture in any medium is a challenge, but in textiles possibly more than most. Rendering body form, skin tone and facial details in cloth and stitch is challenging but it can also be very rewarding.

As a fine art student, I remember drawing plaster busts as a discipline, which I found both daunting and at times boring, although it's something I'm glad of now as it gave me the confidence to approach portraiture as a subject matter. Using a wide-ranging selection of artists and makers who use portraiture in their work, as well as examples from my own practice, my aim is to set out accessible approaches to adding people and figures to your pieces, too.

As a tutor whose practice has most recently spanned the extraordinary Covid pandemic, I have been struck by my students' desire for connection with their environment, pets and home. In recognition of this, I have added an additional short section on pet and animal portraiture.

In **Chapter 1: Selfies at Home**, we will look at self-portraits in a variety of settings. Being able to draw the outline of a face and place features inside it enables us to capture a likeness – using a suitable range of colours and textures makes it easier to visualize. Starting with a good likeness enables further experimentation.

Throughout history, textile portraits have been used to represent social, political and cultural trends and ideas, and artists have taken to stitch to get their message across, as we will explore in **Chapter 2: Representation and Culture**. By using local and personal materials, these images and their meanings are made clear. With examples from artists around the world, this chapter will reflect upon and engage the maker with ideas for self-expression.

One of the joys of making in textiles is the variety of styles to be discovered in artists' works. Portraits enable us to find ways of telling personal narratives with unique interpretations, as we will discover in **Chapter 3: Stylized Imagery**, which also features projects in 3D, including making textile dolls.

Old photographs can be an emotional and richly rewarding resource for makers, as we will review in **Chapter 4: Place and Time**. Capturing an image and place together using portraiture as a subject creates insightful and unique pieces. By using vintage textiles and various photo transfer techniques, I will illustrate how it is possible to create your own 'Moving Memory' piece.

Chapter 5: Narratives is about using ephemera and sourced imagery to create special textile projects and gifts. Combining paper and textile is a popular choice and I will be presenting a variety of approaches here. Adding text or creating work around a piece of writing is a popular source of inspiration for textile artists. Covering an object with portraits and related imagery will also be covered in this chapter.

The final short section of the book is entitled **Pets and Animals** and is all about using animal imagery in textile work. Some practical suggestions and tips for capturing birds, animals and pets in cloth will be explored with projects that will hopefully inspire you to start your own creations.

'Every portrait that is painted with feeling is a portrait of the artist, not of the sitter.'

Oscar Wilde, Irish writer

Above: Anne Kelly in her studio.

Opposite: Anne Kelly, self-portrait in studio.

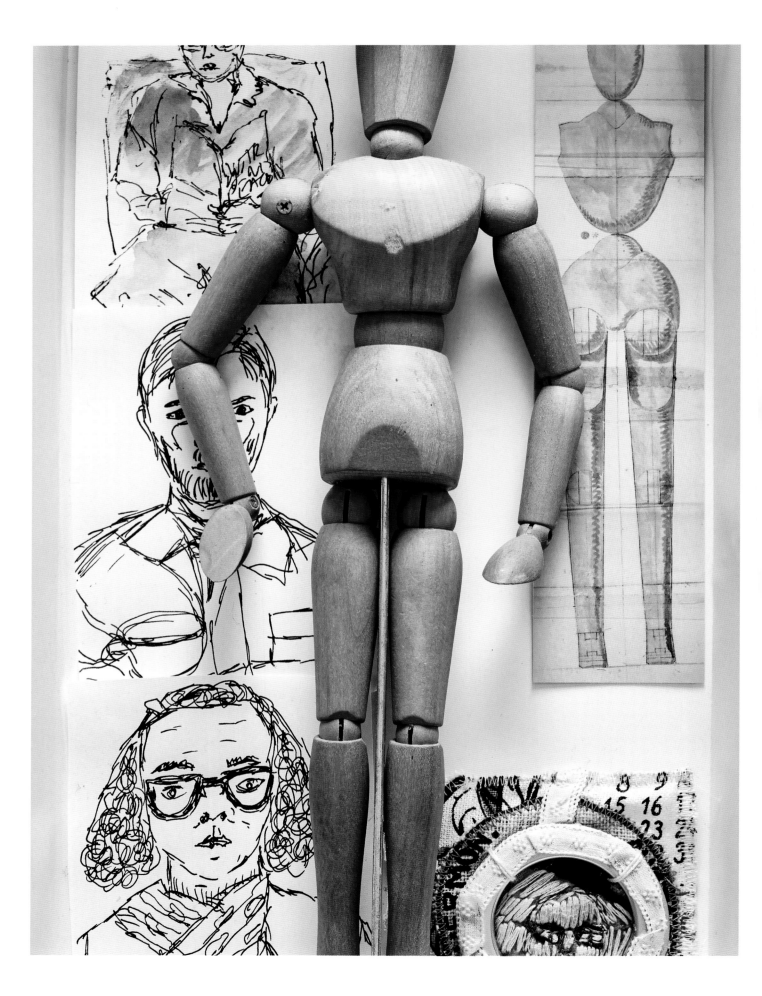

Chapter 1

Selfies at Home

'The tool of every self-portrait is the mirror. You see yourself in it. Turn it the other way and you see the world.'

Agnès Varda, French filmmaker

Anne Kelly, *Tools for Selfies*, mixed-media inspiration board.

Self-Portraits

The global Covid-19 pandemic of recent years truncated our activities by necessity, and home has become a focus for many aspects of our lives. As well as introspection, it has served perhaps to let us focus more deeply on our relationships. In this chapter we are starting with self-portraits and family pictures, not just in the traditional sense but also as indicators of our mental and physical relationships.

I find the easiest way to prepare for making a portrait in stitch is to begin with a drawing. Whether made from life or by using a photograph, it is always a great starting point, and enables you to make notes on details such as skin tone and hair, clothing, lighting and posture. In Portraiture 101, I provide some simple tips for drawing faces (start small, then progress to a larger scale when you feel more confident), while Making a Self-Portrait on Cloth offers a step-by-step guide to help ease you into the making process, including mixing skin tones to add colour, which certainly can be daunting.

From there, we'll be looking at artists who use line to create stitch portraits, starting with the family theme. How to plan and create meaningful compositions while looking at faces and features will also be covered, as will artists who use colour for further definition. Adding colour to portraiture can be complex but rewarding, bringing depth and texture to work, enabling the artist to highlight features in both the portrait and the surroundings. A personal take on self-portraiture and interiors is explored, too.

Below: Anne Kelly, *Self-Portrait* (detail), mixed-media textile on canvas.

Below right: Anne Kelly, sketchbook pages, mixed media on paper.

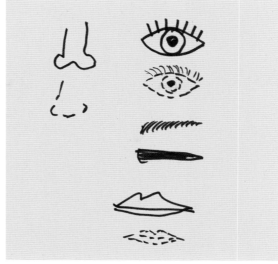

Far left: Anne Kelly, self-portrait, pen on paper.

Left: Anne Kelly, drawings for eyes, nose and mouth, pen on paper.

Below: Anne Kelly, self-portrait with background, pen on paper, and skin tone samples, acrylic fabric paint on paper.

Portraiture 101

Start with an outline of the **face**:

» Notice the face shape – is it round or more oval?

» Ears are located about halfway down the head.

» The top of the eyelid is parallel to the top of the ear.

Locate the **eyes, nose** and **mouth**:

» Draw a faint dotted line down the centre of the face, and draw two lines across to divide the face into thirds.

» The spacing between the eyes is important, as is that between the nose and mouth.

» Draw the features in tentatively to start with, then more firmly when you are happy with them.

Making a Self-Portrait on Cloth

To make a self-portrait on cloth, you will need a photo or drawing of your head and shoulders and an A4-sized piece of calico or sheeting fabric. Equip yourself with acrylic or fabric paints and a mixing palette to experiment with mixing up your skin tone colour.

1 Take the image of your head and shoulders and use a marker pen to draw around the main lines of the portrait.

2 Trace it onto the fabric with tracing paper, then outline the face with a waterproof pen.

3 Mix up your skin tone colour, referring to the skin tone samples (right). For lighter skin tones, use white as a base; for medium and dark tones, use a peach or beige. Add a hint or more of yellow, pink or brown as required. Test on a scrap of fabric or paper, and dry it off to see the finished colour.

4 Once you are happy with your skin tone colour, paint your face in first, using brushstrokes that go in the direction of the shape of the face. Add red or pink to the base tone to create cheek and lip colour. Paint the eyes in, using a small brush to create eyebrows.

5 Stitch around the main outlines of the face by hand or machine. For hair, you can couch wool, silk or string, or use machine embroidery. Add stitching details on the face with long hand stitches or machine stitching.

6 For the background, add collected fragments or pieces of fabric. In my *Self-Portrait*, I have added a piece of needlework, some silverwork and some scraps of cotton fabric.

7 Once the piece is complete composition-wise, you can add extra machine stitching and hand-stitching details as desired.

Above: Anne Kelly, *Self-Portrait*, mixed-media textile on canvas.

Opposite, left: Joetta Maue, *Mother and Child*, mixed-media textile (detail).

Opposite, right: Joetta Maue, *Mother and Child*, mixed-media textile.

Joetta Maue: Mother and Child

Joetta, an American artist based in Boston, has created beautiful 'Mother and Child' stitch sketches showing her everyday family life, as she explains:

'Inspiration comes from being an astute observer of my everyday life. My eyes are always turned on for small moments of beauty and awe in the day to day. I look toward the landscape of my home as muse and document the moments that occur within that space. My thread drawings often focus on the relationships and intimacy of the home space. As I became a mother it was inevitable that my subject shifted to some of the aspects of motherhood.'

'The narrative portraits often focus on the moments of closeness in these relationships. It starts with me noticing a moment that is profound but simultaneously ordinary. I then photograph it and work from the photograph to create a drawing with thread. I used to work more directly from the image, whereas now I work quite intuitively once the basic lines are established, responding to the line and light quality that the original image has. It is a slow, meditative labour that builds love, devotion, repetition and care directly into the piece. I primarily use found domestic linens so that they can bring their own witnessing of the home into the work.'

Holidays

Time spent away or travelling gives us a new perspective on our relationships and breathing space to reflect. When my children were young, we were fortunate to visit a cabin in rural Canada in the summer, visiting family and friends in my native country. Before the invasion of the internet and mobile phones, reading and drawing were activities indulged in between swimming in the lake. *Summer Holiday* captures that place and time, and I used a series of portraits taken from sketchbooks made at the time.

Left: Anne Kelly, portrait sketches for *Summer Holiday*, watercolour and pen on paper.

Below: Anne Kelly, study for *Summer Holiday*, paint and stitch on cloth.

Above: Anne Kelly,
Summer Holiday
(detail), mixed-media
textile.

Right: Anne Kelly,
Summer Holiday,
mixed-media textile.

Family Spaces

In this composite portrait, I combined individual images of my immediate family, stitched over a multi-layered and patched background. I used domestic textiles and family fabrics for the background. I wanted the faces of the family members to be superimposed over the textiles. I used the tracing method as described in Making a Self-Portrait on Cloth (see pages 11–12) to draw the outlines and hand stitched them using backstitch and perle cotton.

Above: Anne Kelly, *Family Portrait*, mixed-media textile.

Above right: Anne Kelly, 'Tom', *Family Portrait* (detail), mixed-media textile.

Right: Anne Kelly, 'Ruth', *Family Portrait* (detail), mixed-media textile.

Dream Portraits

During the first Covid-19 lockdown of 2020 in the UK, I was invited to participate in a fundraising exhibition called 'Isolated Observations' at the Candida Stevens Gallery in Chichester in the south of England. I chose to enter four 'Dream Portraits' based on the strange and disconnected dreams that I was having at the start of the pandemic. I began the portraits as described in Making a Self-Portrait on Cloth (see pages 11–12) but added small objects in the background that connected with the people represented. As can be seen from the two examples featured here, the pieces were made with much extra stitching on top, where I tried to make the lines reflect the contours in the subjects' faces, and additional embellishment in the backgrounds.

Above right: Anne Kelly, *Dream Portrait – Horse*, mixed-media textile, framed.

Right: Anne Kelly *Dream Portrait – Dog*, mixed-media textile, framed.

Emily Jo Gibbs: Kids Today

Emily is a British textile artist based in London. In her 'Kids Today' project, she takes an affectionate look at the children in her neighbourhood, as she explains:

"'Kids Today' is a series of small portraits of children who play in our street. I live on a cul-de-sac in south-east London and very unusually lots of children, including my two boys, play games together in the street. They ride bikes and roller-skate and dress up and make movies. They climb lampposts and kick balls and fall out and make up. They have picnics and water fights, and they grow up together. In this series of work they are all sat at my kitchen table, most eager to take part in the project, some less sure but keen not to miss out.'

Above: Emily Jo Gibbs, *Bill*, mixed-media textile.

Above right: Emily Jo Gibbs, *Violet*, mixed-media textile.

Emily's distinctive use of fabric collage, using layers of silk organza, gives her work an ethereal and delicate quality, and she describes her process here:

'The studies are made from multiple layers and pieces of silk organza that are arranged to create a subtle textile collage; this is then tacked together before being hand-stitched. Lots of tiny, coloured stitches pick out folds and patterns in the clothes, the children's features, and hair.'

Andrea Cryer: Drawing with Thread

Andrea is a textile artist based in the south-west of England. I was attracted to her work after seeing a photograph of her studio wall covered in stitched portraits. She explains her technique:

'I use needle and thread as drawing tools to create images which appear from a distance to have been made using pen and ink. A closer look reveals that the marks are all created using stitched lines on fabric. I use a simple domestic sewing machine together with hand stitching. I tend to create my portraits in monochrome, restricting the palette to blacks and grey and using white for highlights. I like to keep my portraits simple and often leave threads hanging loose, to give extra depth and interest to the stitched lines. My work is more about capturing a moment or emotion, rather than being concerned about where the light might be hitting the face or if there are shadows in the background. The portraits are drawings, not paintings. When I add colour, this is usually limited to the background or to an article of clothing that the sitter may be wearing.'

'I enjoy the whole process, from deciding which area of an image should be the starting point for where the embroidery hoop is first placed on the fabric, to whether a flourish of hand stitching is needed to finish the piece. With portraits, I always start with the eyes, because it is crucial to stitch these as accurately as possible, to get a true likeness. This means starting with a small embroidery hoop focusing on one eye area before moving across to the next. As the drawing develops, I move to a larger hoop. Choosing the base fabric is important as the texture can impact the finished drawing. I am currently stitching on recycled woollen blankets, which have felted nicely over time.'

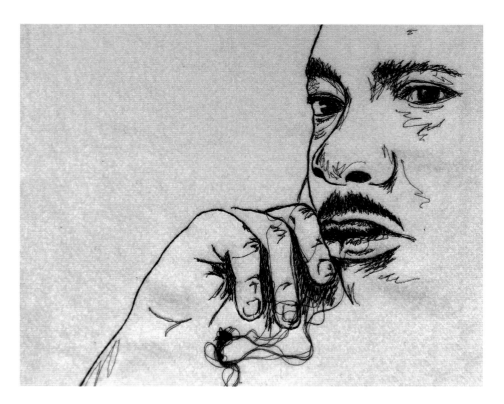

Above: Andrea Cryer, studio 'stitch board', mixed media.

Left: Andrea Cryer, *MLK 2*, stitched textile.

Catherine Hill: A Lancashire Lass

The Covid-19 pandemic meant that many popular stitching shows were cancelled in 2020, including the Knitting and Stitching Shows in the UK; the show organizers decided instead to launch a self-portrait competition, and the entries were exhibited at the 2021 shows in London and Harrogate, as they explain:

> 'At a time when we were unable to greet thousands of visitors at the Knitting and Stitching Shows, the Self-Portrait Competition brought our community together virtually, with a series of textile portraits. Entrants created a self-portrait in a range of textile mediums with a variety of entries received, from cross stitch and embroidery to screen printing and quilting.'

Catherine Hill, a textile artist living and working in Lancashire, a county in the north-west of England, was one of the entrants whose work I wanted to highlight here. She produces striking redwork pieces and has a blog called 'Arnold's Attic', which is very popular and informative, where she writes under the name of Katie.

> 'I am a self-taught embroiderer who uses a needle and thread to capture memory in cloth. As a nod to the county's red rose [the traditional symbol of Lancashire], I often use red thread in my art. Red thread is used once again in *Headspace – Self-Portrait*, a hand-embroidered piece of work created during the second UK lockdown. I used what I had to hand, sourcing an old linen bedsheet and thread from my collection. The initial design for the portrait was hand drawn and developed over several days to incorporate the whirling thoughts and dreams that inspire the creation of my art. Although I'm best known for very small written text, this piece required bigger, more fluid, couched handwriting.'

Catherine Hill, *Headspace – Self-Portrait*, stitched textile.

Diana Springall: A Passionate Collector

Another entrant to the Knitting and Stitching Shows' Self-Portrait Competition of 2020 was Diana Springall, who, like Catherine, makes a valued contribution to our textile community. Diana is a textile artist based in Kent in the south-east of England. Trained at Goldsmiths College, she became a passionate collector of textiles, and in the past has been Chair of both the Embroiderers' Guild and the Society of Designer Craftsmen. Her collection forms an integral part of the new development at the Sunbury Embroidery Gallery in Surrey, as their website explains:

> 'Diana is a revered creative textile embroiderer and practitioner. Through the decades she has extended her time, energy and invaluable knowledge to encouraging others while acquiring an extensive collection purchased from makers, often at a pivotal stage in their career. The sharing of this passion for contemporary embroidery remains Diana's goal throughout.'

Diana's self-portrait was worked from a photo taken by her neighbour, Annette Cartwright. She used felt-covered piping cord, and hand couching stitch in gold and cotton thread. It captures her likeness and vivacity perfectly.

Faith Humphrey Hill: Knit Portraits

Faith Humphrey Hill, *Elena*, knit and print on textile base.

Faith is an American artist based in Chicago, Illinois. Her portrait artwork combines drawing and knitting with digital tools. She describes the process and progression of her striking work here:

'Faces are a fascinating subject. Through them we connect with others. We sense their feelings and learn about their experiences. I enjoy the process of learning about others through visual observation. For this reason, I prefer to use reference photos of real people I haven't met. This allows me to use my eyes to learn about the individual. While creating the drawing I often find myself mirroring the subject's expression, resulting in bringing some of myself into each portrait.'

'Knitting has a vast history that I reference by including it as a layer in my finished artwork. I will at times utilize a non-electric 1950s knitting machine. Machines like mine were invented so women could earn an income from home to support their families. Knitting is a software, and that idea also intrigues me. It has an order and process that is very different from my drawing skills. The knit portraits reference these ideas by introducing knitting for its visual symbolism.'

'Using digital tools was a natural transition that felt authentic to me, given I have lived my life with metal implants in my heart and along my spine. I'm a mix between organic and inorganic, so should my art be. I appreciate how these tools allow me to be portable and not limited by how many colourful supplies I can carry. It enables me to work in layers, introducing different textures and techniques. I love how digital tools allow me to explore scale when exhibiting my work. I work towards embracing the aesthetics of the traditional techniques of knitting and drawing while utilizing all the benefits that digital tools provide.'

'I'm ever curious of the human condition, using my eyes to decode the experiences of others. I want to create a warmth and connection, expose our common thread, using seemingly juxtaposing mediums and processes to create a unified whole. This feeds the viewer's eye with a sense of comfort and togetherness.'

Anuradha Bhaumick: Personal Worlds in a Hoop

Anuradha Bhaumick is an embroidery artist from Bangalore, India, who learnt embroidery at the age of five during a bout of chickenpox. Forced to quarantine her indoors, her mother gave her a handkerchief and taught her lazy daisy, running stitch and chain stitch. Talking about her art practice, Anuradha says:

> 'I wish to embroider the objects that form the patina of one's life story, creating a mini universe and exploring the relationship between a person and their surroundings. I use my mother's kurta scraps to collage my pieces. I have been collecting fabric offcuts for more than a decade. When I use these fabrics in my pieces to appliqué the form of a couch, a blanket, or any other material possession, I am reminded of these heirlooms. I call these fabrics "shona". *Shona* is the Bengali word for gold, and receiving these little pieces of history is precious. My mother has taught me that everything is repairable: a few examples – frocks made of tablecloths, jackets made of old sofa upholstery, quilts made of school uniforms outgrown by her kids – the list is endless. These are what inspire me the most and form the framework of everything I create.'

Above right: Anuradha Bhaumick, *Hey, Soul Sister*, embroidered hoop.

Right: Anuradha Bhaumick, *Terrarium*, embroidered hoop.

Zoom Family Casket

I was inspired by Elizabethan embroidered caskets after seeing one at Penshurst Place, a stately home near where I live in Kent in south-east England. I loved the way that figures were intertwined with elements from the natural world. I decided to create a piece based on my family's communications during the pandemic. I had made small separate embroideries of my family members from screenshots taken during our weekly and much treasured chats.

I found an old sewing box from the 1960s that was solid but needed some refurbishment. I covered the sides with pages from a natural history book and fragments of embroidery taken from pieces that I had found or made. The top was decorated around the main embroideries of my family, with extra pieces of found and made stitched work added to it.

Opposite: Anne Kelly,
Zoom Family Casket,
mixed-media textile on
wooden sewing box.

Above: Anne Kelly,
Zoom Family Casket
(top panel), mixed-
media textile on
wooden sewing box.

Right: Anne Kelly,
Zoom Family Casket,
(top panel detail),
mixed-media textile on
wooden sewing box.

Frances Palgrave: Immersed

Frances is a German textile artist who lives and works in Hamburg. I was drawn to Frances's unique and distinctive self-portrait, *Immersed*, which was exhibited at the 2021 Royal Academy Summer Exhibition in London, although this was not her first self-portrait. A piece entitled *Me* was shown in the Knitting and Stitching Shows' Self-Portrait Competition, as she explains:

'I produced my self-portrait *Me* during the pandemic lockdown. The fabrics I used are keepsakes that reflect on my personal history. Included, too, are stitched images of activities that helped me during that challenging time and which I still enjoy doing now – such as scissors for working with textiles, a pen for writing, or gears for biking. My work *Immersed*

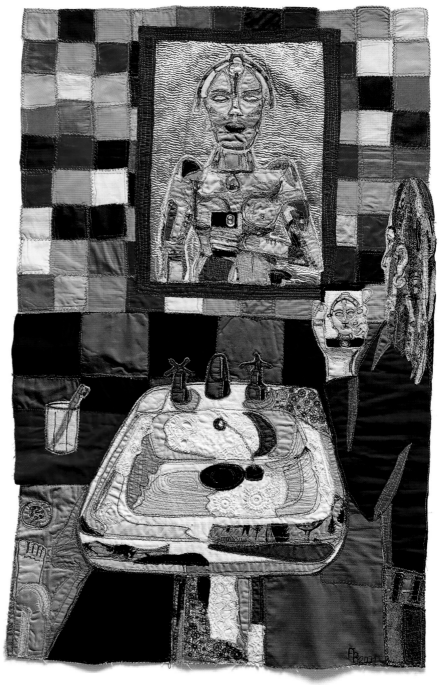

deals with the different shapes of identity we are free to assume – in the real or the digital world. The way I see myself when looking into the bathroom mirror tends to differ from the perception others have of me. Immersing into the digital universe and interacting with a whole new, and largely unknown, community opens up new dimensions for my work and myself.'

'From an initial idea, my free appliqué and textile collages evolve in a long and often meditative journey of cutting, reassembling and sewing. I work with the material on both sides: I start by outlining the image on the back and continue by layering appliquéd fabrics on the front, sewing them back and front. Throughout that process, I try to harmonize the colours and to merge layers of appliquéd fabrics by using free-motion machine embroidery and colourful threads, to fuse the material as well as to thread-paint some details and highlight characteristic features.'

Frances Palgrave, *Immersed*, mixed-media textile.

Suzy Wright: An Eye for Colour

Suzy Wright is a textile artist based in Dorset in the south of England, creating her pieces using free machine embroidery. I saw Suzy's work at the Knitting and Stitching Show, where she was a selected exhibitor. Her gallery was entitled 'The Birds of Paradise Collection'. Suzy herself says:

'I have never hidden away from colour – I always feel it's very easy to run away from it and I try my hardest to embrace it with open arms. As the years have gone by my appearance has become more clashing and vibrant with colour and pattern. I just adore it, it makes me happy, and I don't feel like myself if I wear black. I have always tried to push the boundaries of what to wear. When I was younger, I constantly wore big ballgowns, then it changed to long flowing kaftans and kimonos … I just love how expressive you can be – now I love to wear turbans and wild extravagant hats!'

'I am passionate about my subject, there is no point doing anything unless you are inspired by your surroundings; sometimes that just means going to the garden or to a beautiful vintage clothing shop. I take memories and get images. My watercolours tend to always be massive; I love working big. I pin my painting up on the wall, and I then rip off a large piece of fabric and take pencils and pens and draw quite a detailed version of it in black and white, sometimes changing it depending on how the watercolour has worked. From there I do a base coat of thread, like with a painting, and then build up the layers, until the stitch painting pops out with colour.'

Below left: Suzy Wright, *Self-Portrait*, free machine-embroidered textile.

Below: Suzy Wright, *Self-Portrait*, free machine-embroidered textile (detail).

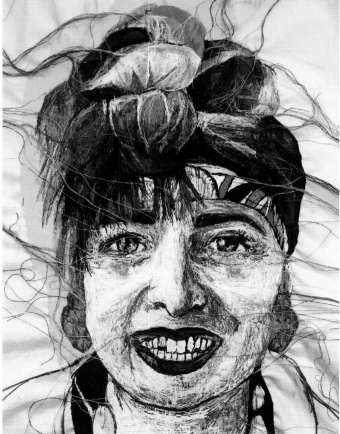

Chapter 2

Representation and Culture

'If you don't try, nothing ever changes.'

Elena Ferrante, Italian novelist

Anne Kelly,
inspiration board,
mixed media.

Getting the Message Across

There are so many ways in which textile art has been and continues to be a force for thought, change and action. Take, for example, the suffragist movement banners created in the early 20th century, used by campaigners (for the right for women to vote in the UK) on marches and at other events. These represented different organizations and are works of art in themselves. They continue to inspire us and to be emulated by contemporary artists and makers.

In this chapter I have focused on textiles that represent political, racial, socio-economic and feminist issues, as well as the portrayal of icons in historic and cultural settings. Facial imagery and portraiture are strong signifiers of identity and can express intention and direction through their depiction in cloth. There is a wide range of media covered in this chapter, all equally effective for making a point.

The viewer on seeing a striking piece, or series, of work can be inspired to look further into a cause or a story, and to even take action. The works in this chapter combine storytelling with artistic interpretation and even, in some cases, provocation. I will also look at the way portraiture can be incorporated into garments and accessories to create an even more powerful message.

Below: Anne Kelly, *Europeans*, mixed-media textile.

Politics and Protest

Starting with politics and protest as themes, the featured work follows the makers' research, thought and interpretations of current or historical events. The materials and processes used are intrinsic to conveying the message in an accessible way.

Europeans

This was the largest and most complex piece of work to be featured in my solo exhibition 'Anne Kelly: Well Travelled' at the Ruthin Craft Centre in North Wales in 2021. Measuring 1.5 × 2m (5 × 6½ft), it was a composite piece, made on a hand-dyed and printed quilt from India. I started by making the central portion by screen-printing the background with a water pattern and then making a map of Europe to go over the top. The side borders were constructed from my '12 Dresses' collection, a series of work exhibited at the UK's Knitting and Stitching Shows in 2019 that represent the women (some of whom perished in the Holocaust) from my father's family. The top centre panel shows portraits of my family. The piece is a statement about migration and travel, and how we are all immigrants. My close family has a European heritage and the piece celebrates our connection with the continent. Words are interspersed in the piece – 'reflect', 'belonging', 'other' – to spark thoughts about citizenship and statehood.

Caren Garfen: Selection

Caren Garfen is an award-winning London-based artist specializing in textiles and painstaking hand-stitching, creating carefully considered pieces with profound messages. Caren's interest has been in gender politics and women's issues in the 21st century. For four years she researched and created artworks relating to the devastating world of eating disorders. However, in 2019, Caren changed direction and is now researching the Holocaust, and examining the shattering rise in global antisemitism. As is her approach, she will delve into all areas of enquiry, trying, once again, to make sense of our complex and problematic world.

Her collection of work entitled 'Selection' focuses on innocent people who were murdered during the Holocaust because they were Jewish. The work is an avowal of remembrance, but also a reminder that antisemitism did not cease when the Second World War ended. On closer examination of 'Selection', there are names, histories and photographs of some of those lost in the 21st as well as the 20th century.

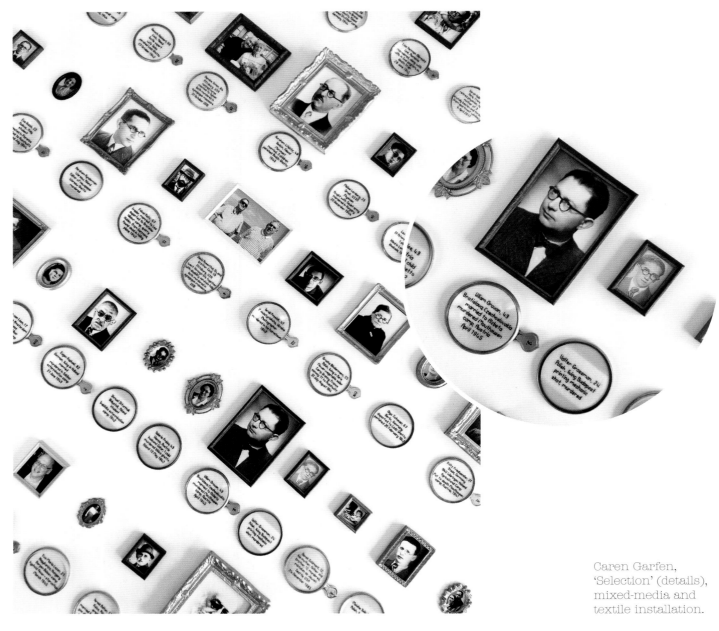

Caren Garfen, 'Selection' (details), mixed-media and textile installation.

Mary Tooley Parker: Gee's Bend Quilters

American textile artist Mary Tooley Parker uses the historic technique of rug-making to create her art. I was drawn to Mary's portraits of the iconic Gee's Bend quilters as they combine details from the makers' quilts with portraits of the makers themselves. Mary recounts how she came to produce these pieces and the process itself:

'I first saw the stunning quilts of Gee's Bend, Alabama, at the Whitney Museum in New York in 2002. I was deeply moved by the exhibition, not only by the visual impact of the quilts, but also by the utilitarian materials that were used to make them. They were examples of the make-do traditions of great folk art, where the maker works with what is on hand, with the simplest of tools, and creates art.'

'Gee's Bend quilts are immediately recognizable and are widely acclaimed as art, but the individual quilters themselves are rarely seen or mentioned. The quilts are not all the same, and neither are the quilters who made them. I wanted to highlight some of the older quilters, whose quilts were really unique and striking, to give them the recognition and respect they deserve as artists.'

Below: Mary Tooley Parker, 'Ma' Willie Abrams, Gee's Bend Quilter, in Klimt, hooked rug wall hanging.

'Working in the simple medium of rug-hooking affords me a strong connection not only to the fibres running through my fingertips, but also to the women who used this medium and other fibre mediums to express themselves during difficult times and with limited materials. Using this medium as a creative expression of my 21st-century experience, I augment this traditional craft with a contemporary aesthetic and take the work off the floor to be viewed as art.'

Right: Mary Tooley Parker, Annie E. Pettway, Gee's Bend Quilter, in Klimt, hooked rug wall hanging.

Far right: Mary Tooley Parker, Sue Willie Seltzer, Gee's Bend Quilter, in Klimt, hooked rug wall hanging.

Suffragist Amelia Scott

I live in the county of Kent in the south-east of England and I am delighted that our new cultural hub in Tunbridge Wells is named after Amelia Scott, a suffragist and founder of the hospital in the town. The hub, which comprises a library, museum and art gallery as well as the town's adult education centre, reopened in 2022. As a tutor at the adult education centre, I was keen to start a project with students involving an aspect of the collection. I knew that the museum had housed an extensive collection of embroidered waistcoats, some of which are now on display in the new hub. The museum staff kindly let my students photograph and draw these waistcoats in their sessions with me. My students then developed their drawings into designs for dresses, and stitched and made the dolls and dresses during their classes. I have included here a couple of those dolls, from students Ruth Lozano and Helen Ott, which were displayed in the Fountain seating area in the gallery. You'll find the pattern for making this doll in Chapter 3.

Anne Kelly, *Amelia Scott Doll*, mixed-media textile and wire, next to a reproduction of a photo of Amelia Scott.

Above left: Ruth Lozano, doll with design work inspired by the waistcoat collection at The Amelia Scott, Tunbridge Wells, Kent.

Above: Helen Ott, doll with design work inspired by the waistcoat collection at The Amelia Scott, Tunbridge Wells, Kent.

Left: Students' work on display in the seating area at The Amelia Scott.

Co-operative Women's Guild Banner

This banner was made in the 1920s for the southwestern section of the Co-operative Women's Guild, formed in 1883 with the aim to spread the knowledge of the benefits of co-operation and improve the conditions of women. It was made after the First World War but is influenced by the suffragist banners which came before it. It is in the collection of the Bishopsgate Institute, an independent centre in London providing talks, discussions and courses for adults. The banner was exhibited at the Embroidered Arts exhibition 2021 at the Oxo Tower in London.

Co-operative Guild Banner, appliquéd and stitched cotton fabric on cotton background, *in situ* at the Hand & Lock Embroidered Arts Exhibition, November 2021.

Claire A. Baker: Gift to My Sister

Claire A. Baker is an embroidery artist based in the north-east of England whose creative practice is inspired by a scattered community of ageing babushkas (grandmothers) who still live in isolated villages within the Chernobyl Exclusion Zone in northern Ukraine, even though the worst nuclear disaster in the world caused this area to be completely evacuated in 1986. Given the recent war in Ukraine, Claire's *Gift to My Sister* is a timely piece, a memorial to the women of Ukraine and their heritage, as she explains:

Claire A. Baker, *Gift to My Sister*, mixed-media stitched textile.

'Through visiting the Chernobyl Exclusion Zone for research purposes over the last six years and investigating the embroidery heritage of a lost community, I have made strong and close relationships with some of the babushkas who still live in this isolated, rural area. During the coronavirus pandemic and lockdown, I started to stitch portraits of some of the women. It was a personal and individual response to my own sense of loss during this period, when I could not visit them due to travel restrictions. Stitching them with what felt like a physical thread between us, I felt more connected.'

'This portrait is of my most favourite babushka and throughout the making, I felt as though I was somehow caring for her. It gave me time with her, and through the act of making I began to make visible my strong attachment to this babushka. There was no initial design, I merely worked over a photograph taken two winters ago, printed onto a linen-like fabric. Using hand-stitching techniques and cotton embroidery floss, I stitched only her face to begin with. However, I had promised I would keep stitching her until we saw each other again and the pandemic kept going. So, I started the background and the piece grew.'

'The pattern was inspired by an early 1980s wallpaper, abandoned in the city of Pripyat where my babushka once lived, pre-nuclear disaster, when she was a nurse at Hospital No. 126. Valentina's favourite thing in the world are her roses and I wanted to include those, so devised the frame. The golden corners are a link to the domestic icons, the religious beliefs and traditions of her everyday life. It also reflects the body of work I was creating at the time – 'Babushka as Icon', in response to my research and describing the strength of feeling I have for these incredible people. I have made work with the babushkas, about them, of them and, ultimately, for them. I presented her portrait to Valentina in Ukraine in September 2021. She said she looks too old.'

James Fox: Reverse Appliqué Rebellion

Scottish-born textile artist James Fox now lives in Lancaster in the north-west of England. His practice focuses on rights and protest. In 'Rights, Riots and Routes', his installation for the 2021 British Textile Biennial at Helmshore Mill, he was inspired by the story of a small piece of cloth cut away from Mary Hindle's dress during the Lancashire loombreaker riots of 1826 and the part it played in her subsequent imprisonment in Lancaster Prison, and this became the starting point for an exhibition that explored the history of protest and punishment. James uses reverse appliqué and banner-making as ways to portray protest in a contemporary and striking way, as he describes here:

'From the loombreaker riots of 1826 through to the 2011 inner-city riots, the working class of Britain have sometimes found themselves in situations where the only way they feel able to voice a protest against such things as unfair wages, poor housing, dangerous working conditions, or no work at all, is the use of insurrection. Mainly using the medium of textiles, and predominantly embroidery, with reverse appliqué I investigate the theme of rebellion and try to unpick the fabric of society.'

'*This Sporting Life* is a comment on the Establishment and privilege. I use the image of a member of the landed gentry dressed in patterns from the countries that Britain has exploited over the centuries. The background is a pattern devised around symbols and icons of the socialist movement in the style of William Morris, symbolizing the struggle as well as the craftsmanship of the working class, who have also been exploited by the so-called elite.'

'*Maintaining the Fabric* is a comment on the 2011 riots, which saw disenfranchised youth take to the streets to loot and cause disorder. After the riots had died down, the Establishment opened up the courts 24 hours a day to make an example of and imprison people for crimes as meagre as stealing one of a pair of trainers.'

Above: James Fox, *Maintaining the Fabric*, reverse appliqué with free-motion embroidery.

Left: James Fox, *This Sporting Life*, reverse appliqué with free-motion embroidery.

Women

Although women have traditionally made textiles throughout history, it is only recently that they have found their voice and told their stories in cloth, sometimes subverting clothing and creating new works in collaboration with other artists.

Willemien de Villiers: Shallow Grave

Willemien is a South African-based textile artist. Her work, composed of images of bodies, words and diagrams carefully stitched onto found fabrics, is intimate, but it is a shared intimacy which – through the unlikely power of vulnerability – forms the basis of a connection between artist and audience. For Willemien, everything is connected, as she explains here:

> '*Shallow Grave* forms part of my 'Domestic' series, which I started in 2017, after a particularly brutal spate of gender-based violence in my country. Statistically, a woman is killed in South Africa every three hours. This is five times the world average. And half of all women murder victims are killed by men with whom they had a close relationship. For me, it became important to honour and remember them the only way I knew – by making art. The female figures I use in my "stitchings" stand in as universal portraits of the dead – an attempt to lay them to rest, to make sure they're not forgotten.'

> 'It seemed fitting to outline the finished work with strips of haberdashery notions – hooks and eyes used when sewing female underwear; to me they're subtle reminders of the many insidious ways women are kept in check, controlled. I like how the metal bits decay and rust over time, adding physical stains to the brutal metaphorical stain and shame of femicide. While researching imagery to use here, I was drawn to symbols of hope, fertility, freedom. I used my favourite stitch, the simple mending stitch, to tell this unknown woman's story. I stitched the text using cross stitch, subverting its more common decorative use.'

Above: Willemien de Villiers, *Shallow Grave*, stitched textile.

Above right: Willemien de Villiers, *Shallow Grave* (detail), stitched textile.

David Morrish: Kingfly Embroidery

David is an experienced embroiderer and lecturer at Sheffield Hallam University in the north of England, and he creates bespoke digital embroideries under the name Kingfly Embroidery. This collaborative piece was his first attempt at creating an all-over digital embroidery for a pre-made garment. Fashion and interiors designer Siobhan Murphy kindly sent him one of her denim jackets to experiment with and to embellish. The piece was showcased on the BBC TV programme *Make it at Market*. David takes up the story:

'We agreed on recreating one of Siobhan's recognizable art pieces, "Donuts are a girl's best friend", with the consensus of going bigger and bolder than a simple image on the centre back of the jacket. My design process had to be reviewed and adapted to turn a 3D garment into 2D shapes that my machine could accommodate. Designing involved both 3D and 2D approaches throughout the process from start to finish. Once the design was initially drafted, it was CAD rendered using a mixture of specialist embroidery software. At this stage the design was further developed and refined, and texture fills applied for effect. As the piece was large it resulted in 35 separate pieces and over one million stitches.'

'For the portrait image, I wanted to create a sense of movement with the hair flowing from the back of the jacket, around the sleeve and finishing at the centre front. The bright pinks, oranges and purples were used with a variety of texture fills and effects to help create a sense of intrigue, depth and detailing. The face contrasted in style and was deliberately more accurate and precise, with fills that followed the contours of the facial features, in an attempt to create a 3D feel. The machine was manipulated during production in order to respond to what was happening at the time, with areas that have skipped stitches or even been overstitched. Though the jacket was initially designed with embroidery on the cuffs, collar and lapels, I later decided that this was too much and that it would distract from the main elements, opting to apply rhinestones to add an extra sense of bling and glamour.'

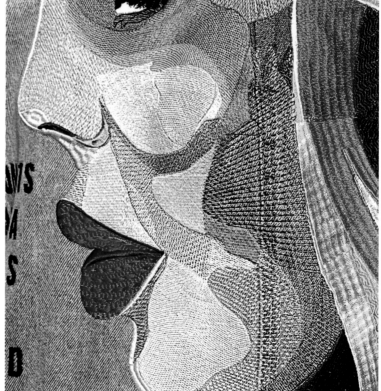

Right: David Morrish, *Donuts Are a Girl's Best Friend*, embroidery on denim jacket.

Far right: David Morrish, *Donuts Are a Girl's Best Friend* (detail), embroidery on denim jacket.

Doll Cat Jacket

In this piece I used a pre-made garment (a small denim jacket found in a charity shop) to make portrait work. In its embellishment I have combined the themes of doll-making and pet portraits, both subjects that I will be exploring later on in this book. I added panels embroidered with drawings of pet cats to each side of the front and to the back of the jacket. I also made an embroidered doll to attach to one of the front pockets. The collar and cuffs were lined with found fabric and this gives the piece a vintage feel.

Above left: Anne Kelly, *Doll Cat Jacket*, mixed-media textile on denim jacket (front panel).

Left: Anne Kelly, *Doll Cat Jacket*, mixed-media textile on denim jacket.

Above: Anne Kelly, *Doll Cat Jacket*, mixed-media textile on denim jacket (doll).

Folk Backpack and Folk Bag

I decided to embellish a small backpack with a figure from South American fabric and embroidered fragments. There was also the addition of a small doll, as well as some extensive hand-stitching around the top edge, and elements of plant embroideries across the piece. This sold at my 'Travelled' show at the Timeless Textiles Gallery in Newcastle, Australia, and I was commissioned to make a bespoke bag using the same elements. *Folk Bag* used a similar template for the main figure, with the addition of insects surrounding it and on the reverse of the bag.

Above: Anne Kelly, *Folk Backpack* (front), mixed-media textile collage on found bag.

Right: Anne Kelly, *Folk Backpack* (reverse), mixed-media textile collage on found bag.

Making an Embroidered Garment or Bag

When trying your hand at making an embroidered garment, it's important to choose an item that you can deconstruct if necessary, and if using a bag, choose a textile-based one.

1 First, prepare your chosen item. Garments should be washed before adding your own design, and for bags, you may need to remove straps and buckles if they are likely to interfere with your stitching – you can always replace them later.

2 It can be useful to make pattern pieces for the item if covering the surface completely.

3 Start with the largest panels first and work towards the smallest.

Above left: Anne Kelly, *Folk Bag* (front), mixed-media textile collage on found bag.

Left: Anne Kelly, *Folk Bag* (reverse), mixed-media textile collage on found bag.

Icons

'Icon' is a much overused word, but how do artists and makers portray famous people in cloth? In this section I am looking at religious-inspired iconography as well as icons of popular culture.

Far left: Michelle Holmes, *The Face of Gabriel*, mixed-media textile collage.

Left: Michelle Holmes, *Material Matters*, mixed-media textile collage.

Michelle Holmes: Portraits of an Angel's Face

Michelle's gallery, Archangel Studio, is deep in the heart of the East Midlands in England. She uses mixed-media textile collage and embroidery to make jewel-like work that resembles painted icons, based on travel and historical textiles, and she describes two of her pieces here:

> '*The Face of Gabriel* – a portrait of the angel's face. The eyes seem very important in this piece. Gabriel is traditionally seen as a messenger, but here Gabriel is thoughtful and silent. Pausing and watching, noticing. The halo is just glimpsed. Jewel-like patterns make up the cloak-like facets of precious materials. The portrait is very still and focused. Fabrics include hand-dyed silk satin for the face, herringbone linen for the hair, Jacquard silk for the cloak, fragments of antique ribbon and crushed silk velvet. Stitches are mostly free-machined with some hand-stitched details.'

> '*Material Matters*, Gabriel again, and I was focusing again on the senses. The ears are particularly important here and have ribbons flowing, drawing attention to them. The angel is focusing on nature and listening to the sounds of the wind blowing across the fields. She is tenderly observing. The background is a cyanotype onto dyed silk satin, the face is silk and the appliqués are in linen and hand-dyed cotton. I used a viscose embroidery thread for the fine features and vintage cotton threads for the hair and background. The hair is a herringbone linen.'

Marna Lunt: Stitched Badge Icons

Marna is an artist based in the north-east of England. In her textile pieces she creates beautiful portraits rich in colour and texture. I am particularly drawn to her badges of famous artists and personalities. They're small but powerful! Describing her process, Marna says:

'When I create work with thread, I approach it exactly as I would if it were paint. I think about the layers, tones, values. I enjoy the mark-making and textures that the thread brings and want those to mimic the brushstrokes and paint textures I would usually build using oil paint. I am not looking to smoothly blend the threads or make a traditional silk embroidery picture. I want blocks of thread to create movement and a tactile surface. I see the thread as simply an alternative medium to watercolours or oils. My style is to be more painterly with my strokes than photorealistic.'

Marna Lunt, stitched badges, hand embroidery on metal frame.

Jenny Hart: Blue Dolly

Jenny is a Midwestern American artist known for her portraiture and for Sublime Stitching, the company she launched in 2001. *Blue Dolly*, her tribute to American singer-songwriter Dolly Parton in stitch, is a folksy design almost reminiscent of a tattoo. She describes this piece and her portraiture process here:

'*Blue Dolly* was completed in 2003. The face, head and torso were sketched on cotton fabric but the rest of the embroidery is free-form. It took two weeks to complete and, initially, I was very unhappy with how it was turning out and nearly gave up. So, to have it become one of my best-known pieces is interesting, but even today few notice that she has blue skin and grey hair. These portraits, which I began making in 2000, have always been inspired by traditional American hand-craft embroidery, the kind you would see only on pillowcases, tea towels or clothing. My artwork is an exploration of various embroidery techniques and styles used in unusual ways. I like playing with imagery that can be very personal and symbolic, but worked in a medium everyone recognizes and responds to. I've really loved seeing how this piece has remained of such interest and how it has inspired so much portraiture in embroidery.'

Left: Jenny Hart, *Blue Dolly*, hand-stitched textile on cotton.

Opposite: Anne Kelly, record sleeve collage for 'Secret 7'' exhibition, mixed-media textile on parchment.

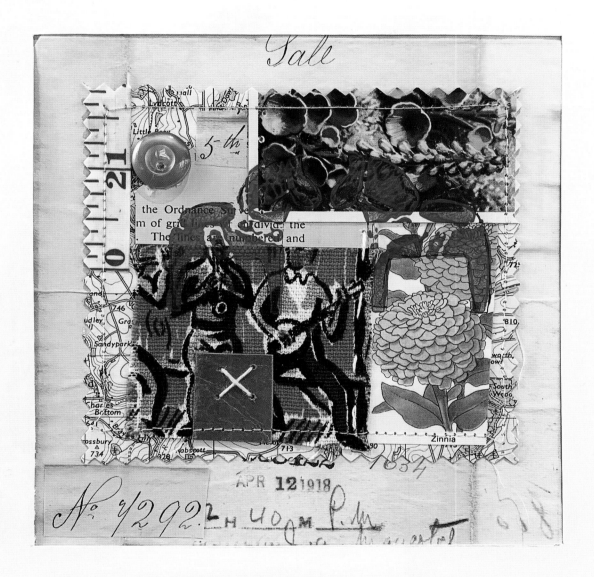

A Musical Collage

'Secret 7'", an anonymous record sleeve sale to benefit the Help Refugees charity, returned
in 2020 to NOW Gallery in the London borough of Greenwich, a space transformed with a
display of 700 records, each with individual sleeve designs. Creatives around the world submit
sleeve artwork creating one-of-a-kind collectables, but these submissions remain a secret until
the records are auctioned and in the new owners' hands. Throughout its history, 'Secret 7'" has
attracted a wide variety of influential contributors. I was delighted to create a design based on
one of the jazz records selected for the competition.

木製ブローチ
こけしさん
Wooden Brooch Kokeshi doll

龍虎謹製

MADE IN JAPAN

PUT 1

Chapter 3

Stylized Imagery

'*Nothing can dim the light which shines from within.*'

Maya Angelou, American author

Anne Kelly, *Doll Collage*, mixed media, featuring artwork from illustrator Sally Welchman (bottom left).

The Doll Form

In capturing the essence of a personality in a portrait, it can often be stylized and simplified. One way of doing this is to focus on recognizable qualities and features, and this can lead to making a three-dimensional form, even as a doll's shape. Dolls can be an emotional release for both the maker and the recipient, as young children continue to show us.

In this chapter I will be looking at the personal interpretation of people in doll form. This will include how to make a doll as well as looking at the doll 'space' as a source of inspiration and display for making. I have deliberately avoided including dolls that are simply decorative, in favour of dolls that reference other sources, meanings or emotions, connecting to other stories.

I hope that this chapter, with an original doll pattern included, will inspire you to try a doll form in your work. When designing my doll pattern, I was keen to create a shape that was simple to stitch and that gave ample room for interpretation. You can decorate and dress the form according to your choice of theme.

Emotional Interpretations

I was inspired to create my *Emily Dickinson Doll* after reading the 19th-century American poet's 'envelope poems', fragments and fragile scraps of writing that are poignant and timely. I found a cloth-bodied doll in a charity shop and adapted it. I describe the process below as a guide to making your own doll artwork.

Left: Anne Kelly, *Emily Dickinson Doll*, mixed-media textile.

Opposite: Anne Kelly, *Emily Dickinson Doll* (detail), mixed-media textile.

Making a Doll by Altering a Pre-Existing Doll

First look for a soft-bodied doll, then choose some cotton fabric for making a garment. In the decoration of my doll, I used fabric paint and a rubber stamp alphabet and embroidery threads of different weights for features and hair.

1 Remove any existing hair and clothing from your sourced soft-bodied doll (alternatively, you can use the doll pattern provided in this chapter to make your own).

2 Make a pattern for a garment for your doll – I used baking parchment and traced it onto plain cotton.

3 Look at your doll's face and decide if you want to change it in any way: you could add colour, or cover the existing features and replace them altogether. I removed the stitched face from my doll and repainted it with fabric paint; I then restitched the features using a photograph of Emily Dickinson for reference.

4 Decide how you want to make the hair – I used long stitches with a heavy embroidery cotton to create mine.

5 Make and decorate the garment according to your theme – I used fabric collage and strips of linen hand printed with rubber stamp letters.

6 Dress the doll with your garment and add any further embellishments to finish it.

Johanna Flanagan: The Pale Rook

Johanna Flanagan is a Scottish textile artist who makes distinctive, beguiling and haunting dolls, which she sees as self-portraits, as she explains:

'For as long as I can remember, I have loved drawing eyes. As a child I would draw eyes – human eyes, animal eyes, eyes from my memory and from my imagination. Whenever I draw a face, I begin with the eyes. I see all of my dolls as self-portraits. Some resemble friends, or children I know, but ultimately they resemble me more than anyone else, even though I've never been able to deliberately draw a convincing self-portrait. All of my dolls have a moment where their character comes to life and it's usually just before I begin to draw their faces. I can see something in the cloth or the stitches that gives me an indication of who they are and what their expression will be, then I merely fill in the details. All of their faces are drawn in a single sitting, and usually it takes no more than a few minutes to tease out who they are in as few marks and pencil strokes as possible. I like to bring them just to the point of realism and no more. I call it the point where they "say hello".'

'No matter how many dolls I create, I can remember where I was and what music I was listening to when they were created. Something of the sense of the place and time always comes through in their face and character. Although their expression is consistently still, the emotion of when they were created and the motivation to create them seems to resonate with others. I'm always fascinated by people's response to them. Some cry, others feel unsettled, but mostly people find them compelling in one way or another. For me, what is important is to create a sense that the doll is utterly present.'

Above: Johanna Flanagan, *Doll*, mixed-media painted and stitched textile.

Right: Johanna Flanagan, *Doll*, mixed-media painted and stitched textile.

Kasia Tons: Explorations in Mask Making

Kasia Tons is an Australian textile artist working with hand embroidery, soft sculpture and wearables, with her work sitting somewhere between art, fashion and craft. Her process is slow and intuitive, with a colourful, loose aesthetic and recurring personal symbolism. She explores universal themes of mental health, technology use and our connection with the environment, one another and ourselves.

Due to their inherently psychological nature, the making of masks has become an important way for her to explore these topics, referencing their use through history to connect the wearer with something beyond or within themselves that is hidden.

Kasia lives and works from an off-grid camp in Peramangk Country.

'*Untitled #3 / Bonnet* was part of my 2020 solo show, "After", at CraftACT [a craft and design centre in Canberra, ACT], responding to an imagined future where digital technology no longer exists and society has to reacquaint itself with the outside world and direct human contact.'

Kasia Tons, *Untitled #3 / Bonnet*, mixed-media soft-sculpture mask form.

Megan Ivy Griffiths: Whimsical Characters

I was attracted to Megan's work and her use of vintage-style imagery in the making of her character dolls.
She describes herself and her practice here:

'I am a pattern designer, illustrator, and embroiderer who is based in the green, glorious Hampshire countryside in the south of England. I harbour an ardent passion for the beautiful and unusual, and I am inspired by whimsical fairy tales and folk costumes from around the world, and calm ambles through forests and fields. My work is a concoction of tenderness, gentility and intricacy. My stitches tell stories; as a trained illustrator, as well as using a pen or pencil, I use a needle and thread to create captivating characters and little companions for everyday life.'

Above: Megan Ivy Griffiths, dolls, mixed media and stitched textile.

Left: Megan Ivy Griffiths, dolls (detail), mixed media and stitched textile.

Making a Doll From a Pattern

I've provided a doll pattern overleaf so that you can make your own embroidered doll from a piece of cotton calico, measuring no less than 30 × 30cm (12 × 12in).

1 Trace or photocopy the cloth doll pattern provided and cut out (note that the pattern includes a 1cm (³/₈in) seam allowance).

2 Fold the piece of cotton calico in half and pin the doll pattern onto the folded fabric, then cut out along the dashed line.

3 Pin the two cut-out doll shapes together and stitch on the stitching (solid) line, starting at the 'X' marked on one side of the head, going down towards the shoulder and all the way around to the 'X' marked on the opposite side of the head.

4 Cut small notches in the seam allowance to enable the fabric to open up better when turning the doll inside out.

5 Using synthetic stuffing or wadding (batting), carefully stuff the doll up to the opening on the doll's head (you may need a long, thin tool such as a knitting needle, chopstick or similar to push the stuffing into the arms and legs).

6 Turn in the seam allowances between the 'X' marks, add a little more stuffing and carefully hand-stitch to close up the doll.

7 Now you can decorate the face and hair using stitch and fabric paints as you choose to.

Right: Anne Kelly,
Annie Doll, mixed-
media textile.

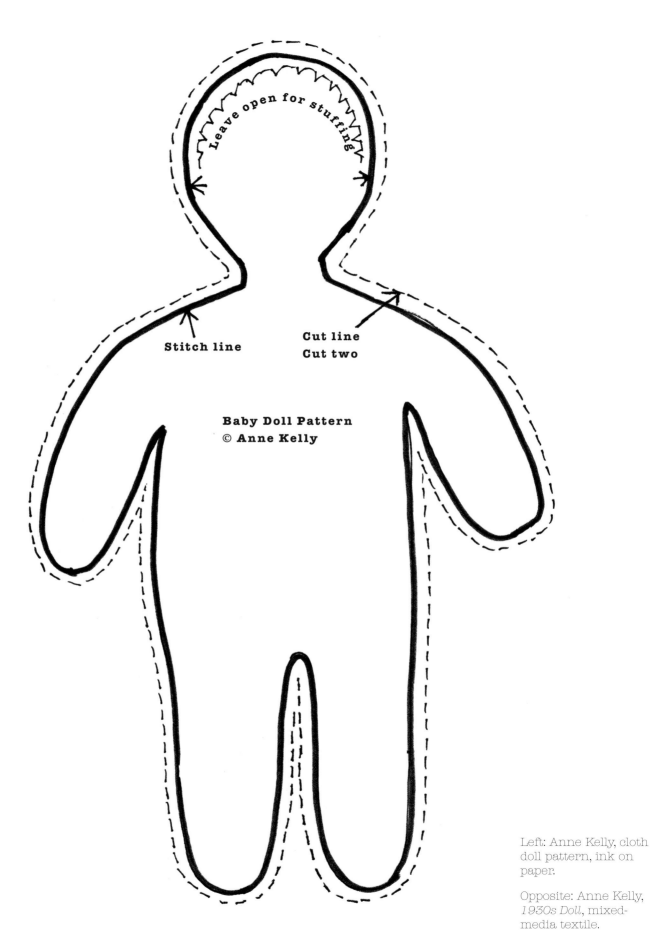

Leave open for stuffing

Stitch line

Cut line
Cut two

Baby Doll Pattern
© Anne Kelly

Left: Anne Kelly, cloth doll pattern, ink on paper.

Opposite: Anne Kelly, *1930s Doll*, mixed-media textile.

Sarah Young: Folktale Inspirations

The work of English artist Sarah Young crosses traditional boundaries of art and craft – she is a painter, illustrator, designer, printmaker, maker in mostly textiles and ceramics, and originator, together with Jon Tutton, of a travelling puppet theatre. Her work is often narrative-based, drawing on folktale, myth and fairy tale, and it has been shown in galleries throughout the UK.

Sarah makes one-off dolls from vintage and recycled fabrics and materials, and she describes one of her creations here:

> '*Mossycoat* is a Romani folktale very similar to Cinderella. This is the third of the three dresses that feature in her story, a mossy coat made of moss and gold threads. This was the first time I used needle punch. *Mossycoat* is made from vintage silk threads, stamens and reindeer lichen.'

Sarah Young, *Mossycoat*, mixed-media textile doll.

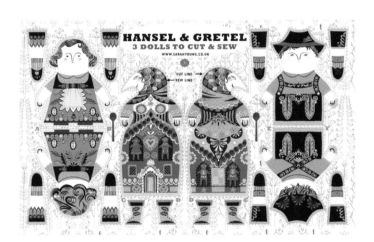

Sarah has also designed a series of cut-and-sew kits, including 'Hansel and Gretel', which she describes here:

> 'It is one of 14 different designs. It is silkscreen printed onto 100 per cent cotton. It can be used as a tea towel or, following the easy printed instructions, the three dolls can be cut out, sewn and stuffed to make Hansel, Gretel and the Gingerbread Witch. The front of the witch lures the children in with sweets and biscuits but turn her around and her true intentions can be seen: the gingerbread twins are transformed into skeletons.'

Above left: Sarah Young, 'Hansel and Gretel', silkscreen printed pattern on cotton.

Left: Sarah Young, 'Hansel and Gretel', stitched and filled.

Melanie Bowles: Stitch-School Dolls

The Stitch-School Doll embroidery kit is designed by Melanie Bowles and there are two designs to choose from, 'Hope' and 'Joy'. Stitch-School, based in south London, designs embroidery kits to inspire the study of stitch with a playful approach, for all ages to enjoy the art of needlework. 'Hope' and 'Joy' were inspired by folk embroidery, and based on the shape of the Russian matryoshka doll with a nod to Clothkit dolls of the 1970s, when domestic and households crafts were very popular.

Melanie designed the dolls during the lockdown period of the Covid pandemic in 2020 when there was a resurgence of and interest in craft activities. She believes the act of embroidery is an antidote to fast modern life, offering a creative activity to escape from digital screens, a chance to slow down, to learn and to relax. The intention is to create an enduring object that will hold family narratives and that will be enjoyed by all generations and cultures, as well as keeping the act of stitches alive and appreciated. Available on the Stitch-School website, they were also sold at the Hayward Gallery shop at London's South Bank Centre as part of the 'Louise Bourgeois: The Woven Child' exhibition in 2022.

Above: Stitch-School Dolls, 'Hope' and 'Joy', mixed-media textile (filled and stitched).

Left: Stitch-School Dolls embroidery kit, mixed-media textile.

Dolls' Heads Inspired by Louise Bourgeois

I was completely blown away by the 'Louise Bourgeois: The Woven Child' exhibition at the Hayward Gallery in 2022, the first major retrospective of the French-American artist's work to focus exclusively on her use of fabrics and textiles.

One of the best ways to gain experience of drawing figures is to use sculpture – indeed, I remember drawing plaster busts at art college. I made a series of sketches of Louise Bourgeois' work with figures, to use as inspiration for a series of dolls based on her exhibition as well as for other projects.

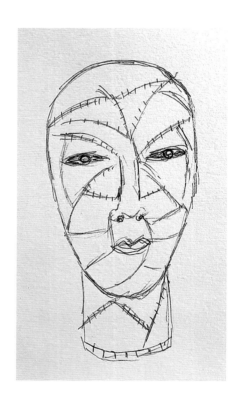 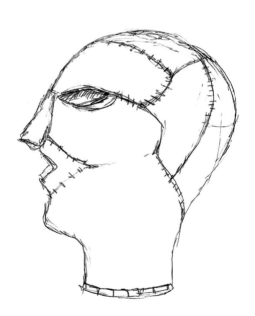 

Above and opposite, above: Anne Kelly, drawings from the Louise Bourgeois exhibition, Hayward Gallery, 2022.

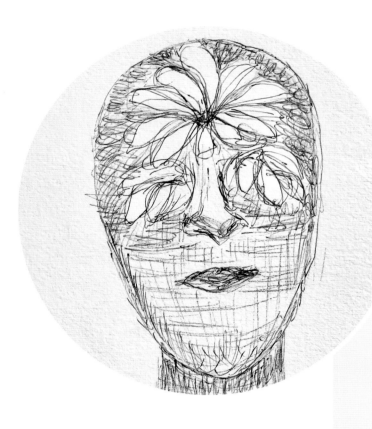

Below: Anne Kelly,
*Louise Bourgeois
Inspired Doll*, porcelain
head and textile body,
mixed media.

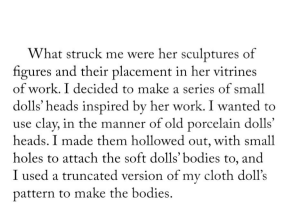

What struck me were her sculptures of figures and their placement in her vitrines of work. I decided to make a series of small dolls' heads inspired by her work. I wanted to use clay, in the manner of old porcelain dolls' heads. I made them hollowed out, with small holes to attach the soft dolls' bodies to, and I used a truncated version of my cloth doll's pattern to make the bodies.

Lynne and Michael Roche: Roche Dolls

Lynne and Michael have an established and well-regarded doll-making practice in Bath in south-west England and I met them when tutoring at the Bath Textiles Summer School. It is fascinating how they have combined their skills of woodworking, porcelain moulding and textiles to create internationally collected dolls. Lynne describes her approach to doll-making and one specific new doll here:

'The doll's name is Esme. She has porcelain head and hands and a fully articulated limewood body. We have been making dolls for over 40 years, firstly inspired by the beautiful French dolls of the 19th century, then going on to model the heads ourselves. The dolls have to be articulated and the clothes must be able to be changed – in other words, they can be played with … by people of any age! They are not fixed, to be put in a cabinet like a sculpture.'

'I love detailing in the clothes and enjoy using natural materials, linens, cottons and yarns … The clothes aren't really contemporary, maybe nostalgic and rather timeless. Hand embroidery has always been very interesting to me, and enriched by learning more of the very old techniques.'

Above: Lynne and Michael Roche, *Esme*, wood, porcelain and stitched textile.

Above left: Lynne and Michael Roche, *Esme* (detail), wood, porcelain and stitched textile.

Louise Asher: A Doll Space

I have had the privilege of working with English artist Louise at her former business, Hope & Elvis. She is now based in the seaside town of Margate in Kent. Her work is minimal in look and inspired by collections, especially of her beloved dolls. She makes installations with them, and her work often develops from these, as she describes:

'My love of dolls and dolls' clothes really came to the forefront when I had children – the random limb in the bottom of the toy box at playgroup and the discarded pair of ripped Barbie tights, they needed to be mended, repaired, repurposed; I couldn't leave them behind. I combine my passion for textiles and embroidery with plastic doll parts found in charity shops, antique markets or kindly gifted (I'm getting a little bit of a reputation!).'

'I'm drawn to the colour palette that dolls bring, from faded oranges and pinks to vibrant blues and reds of the eyes and lips. My favourite finds are the vintage dolls' faces; their expressions tell so many stories. I don't ever start with a plan, sometimes it's just a feeling when sorting in the boxes. I let the materials let me know who they are.'

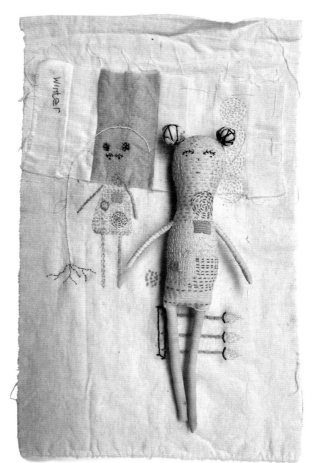

Above right: Dolls in Louise Asher's studio space.

Right: Louise Asher, dolls, stitched textiles.

Left: Louise Asher, background and doll form, stitched and collaged textiles.

Doll Collections

Dolls can be inspiring for sketching and observational drawing, as the pages of my sketchbook attest to. In the doll collections shown here, I have chosen three very different dolls from world cultures and paired them with a variety of my textile pieces.

Anne Kelly, 'Russian Dolls', sketchbook pages.

Above: Gujarati doll on Anne Kelly folk landscape.

Above right: Italian doll on Anne Kelly folk canvas.

Right: Kokeshi doll on Anne Kelly house folder.

A Doll's Case

I was inspired to make a doll's case from a small cardboard luggage case found in a charity shop. It reminded me of a case that I used to keep my dolls in when I was a child. I used a vintage 1975 tea towel to decorate the background and made figures of my sister and myself from that same year. They were drawn from photographs and stitched onto calico backed with blanket cloth, using free-motion machine embroidery on coloured backgrounds. I trimmed the edge of the box with vintage ribbon and a tape measure. The box was lined with old book pages and varnished.

Above: Anne Kelly, *1975 Case*, mixed-media textile collage on vintage case.

Opposite: Anne Kelly, *1975 Case* (detail), mixed-media textile collage on vintage case.

Chapter 4

Place and Time

'You can't sit around and wait for somebody to say who you are. You need to write it and paint it and do it.'

Faith Ringgold, American painter

Nostalgia

Capturing likenesses in cloth can also be about preserving places and memories in time. Many textile artists use old photographs, ephemera and research from locations and events to create meaningful artworks. Often it is a single fragment that can trigger or recreate an emotion or thought. In this chapter I will be looking at work that not only memorializes but also seeks to tell us about our identities.

Photographs can be very useful not only for reference when making work about people, but also as part of the work itself. I will show you how to draw from photographs and how to use photo transfers too, as the basis for new pieces of work. It is a good way to preserve family images or personal memories, as I will demonstrate in Making Moving Memories later in this chapter (see pages 76–77).

Using photographs as imagery to stitch onto can also be useful in creating meaningful artwork. I will be looking at artists who make works using whole photographs, chosen for their impact and artistic merit. It is helpful to see the ways in which these images are altered and given a new perspective with the interventions that these artists make.

Top: Anne Kelly, *Outside 1*, mixed-media textile.

Above: Anne Kelly, *Outside 1*, mixed-media textile.

Making a Start with Photographs

Memory is a powerful emotion and can be the catalyst for making pieces with depth and richness. Looking through old photographs in particular can be empowering and they can provide many opportunities for new work.

1 You will need clearly defined photographs of your person(s). Choose photos that are clear, so you can see as many details as possible. Once you have made your final choice, take a copy of the photo or scan it in black and white, and enlarge it.

2 Trace the section of the photo that you wish to use, then retrace the outline onto tracing paper so both sides are marked.

3 Trace the outline image onto a piece of calico or untextured linen larger than your photograph, keeping it in place with masking tape to prevent it from moving.

4 Mix up your acrylic or fabric paint colours (see Chapter 1: Making a Self-Portrait in Cloth) and paint in the figure.

5 Cut out the painted figure and attach to a background fabric, stitching in the details of the face, hair and body either by hand or machine.

My Sister and Me

I was sorting through some family photographs and found a lovely photo from the 1960s of my sister and me with our toy dolls at my grandmother's house in London. I had been given some quilter's 'hexie' scraps that reminded me of those days and decided to use them as a background. I painted the figures as described in Making a Start with Photographs (see page 71) and incorporated them into the piece of work. The textiles were mounted on canvases.

Above left: Anne Kelly, *My Sister and Her Doll*, mixed-media textile.

Above: Anne Kelly, *Me and My Doll*, mixed-media textile.

Darren Ball: Model Inspirations

Darren is a London-based textile artist whose figurative work is largely inspired by his collection of vintage *Stitchcraft* magazines, as he explains:

'After being given a number of the magazines from the 1940s, I became interested in the photographs and drawings of the models and the way in which they capture the fashions and social history of the period. Seen now, the photographs appear to have humour because of their stereotypical representations of men and women. I use vintage handkerchiefs and coasters to form the canvas for my embroideries because they are so evocative of the period. I respond to the individual qualities of the fabrics, selecting photographs from the magazines to suggest possible narratives.'

'My work is domestic in scale to reference the size of the magazines and the domestic nature of the knitwear. I use a found palette of collected fabrics, aiming to draw and paint with textiles. The mark-making is achieved through free embroidery, contrasting surface qualities of fabrics and embellishment. I work in fabric and embroidery because of its relevance to my subject matter and because the marks created are specific to it.'

Above left: Darren Ball, *Matinée Idol*, mixed-media textile on cotton.

Left: Darren Ball, *Bruce*, mixed-media textile on cotton.

Above: Darren Ball, *Roger*, mixed-media textile on cotton.

Jenni Dutton: The Dementia Darnings

Jenni is a multimedia textile artist based in the south-west of England who is especially noted for 'The Dementia Darnings', a series of work exhibited at the Knitting and Stitching Shows in 2018, which she describes here:

'They were developed from my mother's interest and joy in looking through the family photo albums. She was diagnosed with dementia in 2005 and as my role as her carer increased, it seemed only possible to continue my practice by making her, and our situation, the subject of my work. *Mum with a Spotty Bow* was the first in the series. I have used an iconic image of Mum from her youth and developed the image in a way similar to making a cross-hatched drawing, by sewing through fine dress netting stretched over a 130 × 90cm (51 × 35½in) canvas. Whilst making this piece, I masked off areas of the canvas and the photo so I could concentrate on small areas without being distracted by the whole. I turned both upside down so I could further dissociate myself from such a familiar image and just concentrate on the visual elements. It is a tactile, meditative process.'

'I enjoyed using materials traditionally associated with the feminine, the domestic, whilst honouring the mother/daughter relationship. The work is also about time; the split-second to capture a photographic likeness is reproduced slowly using wools over a couple of months. The long, dangling threads signify the inevitable unravelling of memory over time, the loss of self.'

'Making "The Dementia Darnings" has been a process of emotional repair. Over ten years I have made 16 portraits in the series as I traced the transformative effects of dementia to my mum's death in 2015.'

Jenni Dutton, *Mum with a Spotty Bow*, mixed-media stitched textile on canvas.

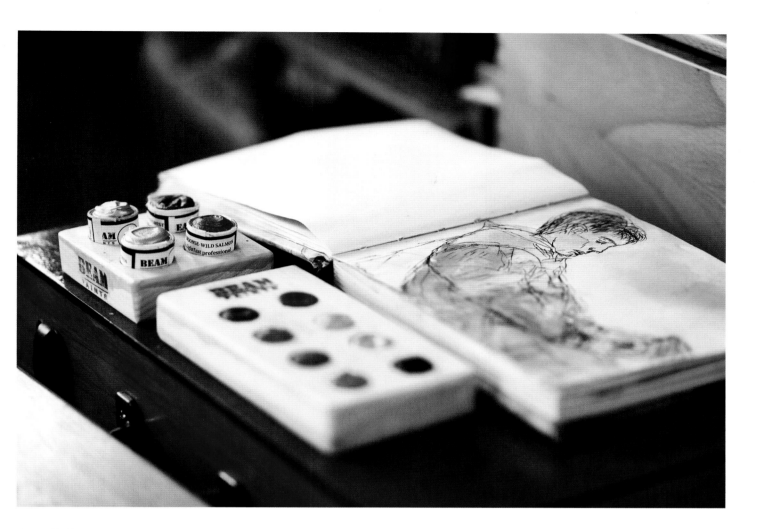

Anne Kelly,
sketchbook and
paints, in studio.

Photographs as Fragments and for Stitch

The use of photographs or sections of photographs, and ephemera with photographs and fragments of them, can be quite powerful and effective in textile work. Photographs are great surfaces for stitching onto when combined with fabric. The key is how to treat them and stitch them while protecting precious originals. There are several ways to do this including:

» Photo transfers, photocopying/printing onto fabric prepared for use in a printer

» T-shirt transfers, available in use for light or dark fabrics

» Preparation with an acrylic-based solution (PVA diluted) or acrylic wax (as described in Making Moving Memories: see pages 76–77)

Making Moving Memories

Travel, memory and collections remind us of places we have been or would like to visit. Here we look at how to make a personal and meaningful repository for a special place (actual or imagined) of your choice. We will be using printing, fabric collage, fabric and paper lamination, and hand and machine stitching.

Selection

Look through your collections, selecting old and new pieces of fabric, ephemera and decorative paper to use for your piece (it's helpful if you choose a colour scheme), and decide on a place, time or family memory that you would like to celebrate. In particular, gather together the following:

» Photographs, sketches and/or ephemera relating to your theme

» An A4/A3 piece of strong fabric, calico or cotton, for background

» An A4/A3 piece of organza (clear) or netting

» Old domestic textile fragments (embroidered or plain)

» Scraps of fabric, old and new – florals and patterns

» Printing blocks (if you have them) relating to your theme, or use cut-up pieces of sponge

» Ribbons and lace and small buttons for embellishing

Anne Kelly, sewing box.

Preparation

Before you start:

» Treat water-resistant paper items with
  a 50/50 mixture of PVA glue and water,
  or acrylic wax

» Cover any old or original photos with
  organza or netting to protect them

» Transfer precious items (photos or
  ephemera) by scanning onto fabric, using
  printable fabric or fabric transfers

» Make prints with printing blocks and sponge
  to add into your work

Anne Kelly, studio wall.

Process

1 Using a large piece of plain or minimally
  decorated fabric as your background, lay
  out your selected pieces onto it, moving
  them around to create balance and taking
  photos with your camera to see if the
  composition works.

2 Once you are happy with the arrangement,
  use a glue stick to lightly glue the pieces
  into place (or pin if preferred).

3 Stitch all loose elements down with little
  stab stitches using a neutral thread.

4 Work from the background to the front of
  the piece, creating texture with repetitive
  hand-stitched patterns (seed stitch, kantha,
  etc.) or using machine stitch.

5 Outline the main elements with free-
  motion embroidery or blanket stitch.

6 To finish, use printing blocks to add
  writing or words if you choose to, or any
  additional embellishments, such as buttons,
  lace and ribbons.

Memory Quilt

When I was in the States, I found a damaged vintage quilt in a shop and decided to use it as a background for small hand-stitched squares: memories of summer and places visited. The details were stitched onto the quilt and kantha stitched around to create a frame. I found the fruit cross stitch pieces in a charity shop and added these to the quilt as well.

Above: Anne Kelly, *Memory Quilt* (detail), mixed-media textile collage.

Left: Anne Kelly, *Memory Quilt*, mixed-media textile collage.

Me and My Toy Dog

This was a collaged piece using fragments from photographs and remnants from the studio. It was made for a group exhibition at the Fibreworks Gallery, near Vancouver, Canada. The show was called 'A Beautiful Mess', and it was all about 'happy accidents', those works made from mistakes in the making process. I was pleased as my composition ended up being about another childhood memory, with the elements arranged in a seemingly random way.

Baby Days

My grandson was born early and had a well-documented journey from the hospital to home with his devoted parents. I received many photos of him at different stages, marking his progress, and I wanted to remember this stressful but ultimately happy time in a textile wall hanging.

I found a vintage quilt top when working in southern France for French General, as well as some children's cotton shirts. We had the opportunity to experience the technique of woad-dyeing from Mariam Lambert, and I dyed several of the little tops.

I used photographs to draw the imagery onto the tops and free-motion stitched into the drawings. They were also hand-coloured and overstitched onto the quilt background. The finished piece was first exhibited as part of my solo exhibition 'A New England Barn' at Cowslip Workshops in Cornwall, in the summer of 2022.

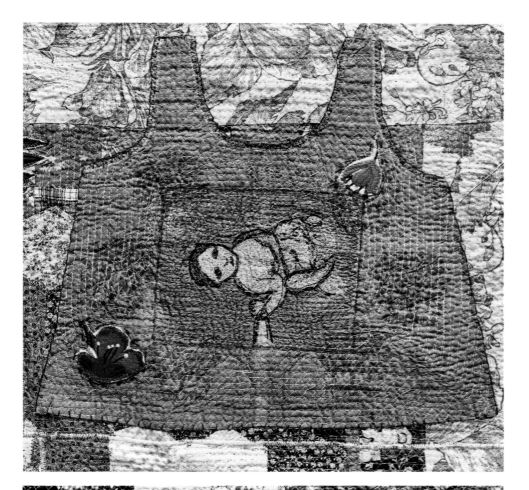

Opposite: Line-drying woad-dyed pieces at French General workshop, southern France.

Right: Anne Kelly, *Baby Days* (details), mixed-media textile.

Maria Thomas: Capturing the Moment

Maria is an English quilt artist based in the Midlands whose use of found imagery and photographic references in collage make original, colourful and inventive works. She had an exhibition of these pieces at the Knitting and Stitching Shows in 2021. She describes her practice here:

'My textile art is all about mixing it up. I call myself an alternative quilter and love to salvage and gather up all sorts of redundant objects to use in my work. Together with memories, found objects, fabric and daily ephemera, I combine different weights of cloth, paper and objects in no particular order. I simply observe how the mix of materials interrupt each other when side by side. Transforming my finds through textile collage, my approach is to compose and balance the visual imagery I find – a bit like drawing. Choosing to work with the traditional methods of hand patchwork and quilting, I make textiles slowly and with much contemplation, combining all found elements together, piece by piece.'

'I make to capture a moment and like to re-use fabrics and found objects that have had a previous life. I am inspired by memories and I'm instinctively drawn to quilted textiles and the comfort they offer. For me, it's all about association. The objects I find inspire my work – mementos from a moment in time, they are the key to my creativity. Using them as memory triggers, I like to rehouse and connect them together with collage and stitch. Often, I will gather items a long time before they materialize into a piece. The traditions of patchwork, quilting and garment-making give me working methods with rules that I can break and a structure I can play with whilst I create a visual response.'

Above: Maria Thomas, *Three Spoons a Day* (detail), mixed media and found textiles, collaged and stitched.

Left: Maria Thomas, *Free-Range Egg Custard Tart* (detail), mixed media and found textiles, collaged and stitched.

Melissa Zexter: Unreproducible Photographs

Melissa, an American artist based in Brooklyn, New York, combines photography and embroidery as part of her practice. Her sketch-form and expressive stitching creates texture and layers in her work, as she explains:

'I sew by hand directly onto photographs I have taken, combining a traditional practical skill, embroidery, with a modern and mass-reproducible process, photography. My fundamental concern is to explore the photograph's material status as three-dimensional object as well as to examine issues of identity, memory and technology. My interest in the creation of unique, hand-crafted, photographic objects is related to the proliferation of images in the modern age, one where images – and specifically photographic images – have lost their own object status altogether. Through manipulations of the image surface, with embroidery or the partial removal of the emulsion, the photographs become unique, and are no longer reproducible objects. Concerned with the interaction between hand and eye in relation to the photographic image, my complex works explore memory and personal experience while manipulating the generic qualities of the photographic print.'

Above right: Melissa Zexter, *Portrait and a Portrait*, mixed-media textile.

Right: Melissa Zexter, *Bluebird by the Window*, mixed-media textile.

Summer Kiser: Stitched Stories

I was fortunate to meet Summer when tutoring at a retreat in Scotland for Wandering Craft Retreats. She helps to organize and run their classes and divides her time between the UK and the USA. She devised this delightful hoop-stitched project, using copyright-free photographs, for the Scottish retreat. Describing her practice, Summer says:

'Although I'm drawn to a diverse range of mediums, textile art will always be my true artistic "home". At our UK-based art retreats (organized with fellow Wandering Crafter, co-founder Jane Bumar), I teach my 'Stitched Stories', combining the time-honoured craft of embroidery with vintage photography. This project interweaves memories of the past with new directions and inspiration.'

'My embroidered designs are diverse and range in style, but I'm always drawn to images that offer a glimpse into a deeper story waiting to be told. Photographs of haunting faces, simple landscapes and people involved in everyday tasks are all waiting to be brought to life with needle and thread.'

'By embellishing historic images collected from flea markets and public-domain collections, a shadowy and long-forgotten character from the past is brought back into focus with clever botanical adornments. Everyday objects are quickly transformed when covered with stitches to form a new, unexpected item. Each thoughtful stitch magically enhances the photo with added colour and dimension, creating a new story.'

Summer Kiser, examples of stitched textile projects with photographs.

Neil Bottle: All That Remains

Neil is a textile artist and tutor based in Kent, south-east England. He describes his original approach to using digital imagery here including the inspiration for his piece *All that Remains*:

'An elegant black and white photograph of my grandmother holding my mother, taken in 1940, was the first element in a series of circumstances and events which formed the inspiration for the 'All That Remains' project. *All That Remains*, the title piece in this body of work, shows this photograph in a complex collage of images depicting some of these elements. In particular, the view from the window of my grandmother's sitting room in her first-floor apartment, which became our temporary home during the refurbishment of our new seaside house. This period of temporary residence fell shortly after my grandmother's death at the age of 96. As I sat on the sofa sifting through her long-stored photographs, where she had once sat stitching her evening dresses, I gazed at that very same view, some 50 years later. I was struck by the memories embedded in this building, both real and imagined. This is where my passion for textiles began and even as a very young child I would sit and stitch beside her, listening to tales of her life during the Second World War, engrossed in the stories and the glamour of the Saturday afternoon films, which flickered on the black and white television in the corner of the room.'

Above: Neil Bottle's research images.

Below: Neil Bottle, *All That Remains*, hand and digital collage, printed wall hanging.

'As a digital artist born in the late 1960s, and with over 30 years of analogue printed textiles experience, my approach to the use of CAD (computer-aided design) is very different to a generation of younger, digital-native designers who have never experienced a pre-digital existence. My lifelong passion for pattern and cloth combined with three decades of working as a print designer have equipped me with an analogue tool kit with which I explore the world of digital design.'

'For over a decade I have pushed the boundaries of computer software in development of my work and in the pursuit of the highest quality digital print resolution available. With the development of the latest generation of digital printers, digitally printed textiles can now rival the quality of hand-printing and even surpass it, with the limitless opportunities it presents for creative expression. Digital production methods are often associated with mass production, but my approach is more similar to that of a painter, building up complex surfaces and layers of imagery, and my creative outputs are carefully crafted, honed, reworked and refined digital one-off pieces, which have required a fluency in the complex language of our digital world.'

28176. Robe en toile ou lainage. Des pinces cintrent la taille. Au dos, fermeture métallique prolongée en pli creux. Col lingerie. (14 à 16 ans. 1 m. 80 en 140. Garniture : 0 m. 35 en 60.) ▧ 28138. En lainage à damiers, jupe en forme et boléro arrondi à [revers. Chemisier de batiste orné de plis. (6 à 10 ans. 1 m. 70 en 140. Chemisier : 1 m. 55 en 80.) ▧ 28168. Une ...... formant poche garnit le devant de cette robe de toile. Col, nœud et revers de lingerie. (11 à 13 ans. 1 m. 80 en 140. Garniture : 0 m. 30 en 90.) ▧ 28... Robe de cretonne imprimée. Un empiècement droit retient, devant et ... ..., groupes de plis couchés. Haut du corsage retourné en revers. (5 à 7 ans. ... en 130.) ▧ 28185. Manteau de drap. Les pinces de la taille se perdent dans les poches appliquées à rabats boutonnés. Au dos, plis ronds sous une ...... gale. (8 à 10 ans. 2 m. 15 en 140.)

PATRONS-MODÈLES
aux âges indiqués
Chacun : 40 fr.
Fco, 50 fr.

28100. Au devant de cette robe de piqué deux panneaux plissés s'incrustent sous des rabats de poches boutonnés. Manches kimono à revers. (8 à 10 ans. 2 m. 40 en 100.) ▧ 28134. Un paletot droit à poches appliquées et une jupe à plis ronds montée dans un corselet composent cet ensemble de lainage ou toile. Blouse assortie. (2 à 4 ans. Blouse : 0 m. 90 en 80. Paletot et jupe : 1 m. 60 en 140.) ▧ 28136. Ensemble en tissu imprimé comprenant boléro à manches longues et jupe à plis ronds. Chemisier en plumetis, froncé sous un empiècement; manches ballon. (5 à 7 ans. Imprimé : 1 m. 45 en 140. Plumetis : 1 m. 30 en 80.)

Imprimerie de Montsouris, Paris.

Le Gérant : J. MAY.

VIEW 2

Chapter 5

Narratives

'After nourishment, shelter and companionship, stories are the thing we need most in the world.'

Philip Pullman, British author

Anne Kelly, Stories, box, mixed media.

Storytelling

Textile artworks can have a unique way of telling stories. Perhaps it is their connection with domestic textiles, engaging with our first impression of cloth and its textures as small humans. They enable us to present tales of everyday events, imaginary worlds, political histories and everything in between. The addition of people, faces and figures makes them even more meaningful.

In this chapter, I am looking at narrative pieces, combining portraiture with working in series, telling stories in cloth and adding text to pieces of work. I am interested in how each of these ways of combining stories and text with people and images can be personalized and made unique. I will also be looking at a couple of exhibitions where portraiture appears front and centre.

Storytelling with portraits is a wonderful way of remembering past events, re-examining your own or others' histories and creating memories using current or past imagery. Portraits attempt to capture the essence of people's natures and present them at a fixed moment in time. This contrasts with, but also complements the narrative form, making it a unique way of creating artworks. Using text in these narrative textiles can be an effective way of emphasizing the meaning and message, giving pieces a context and reinforcing the stories that they tell. This chapter concludes by featuring the work of two artists who use text in very different but equally effective ways.

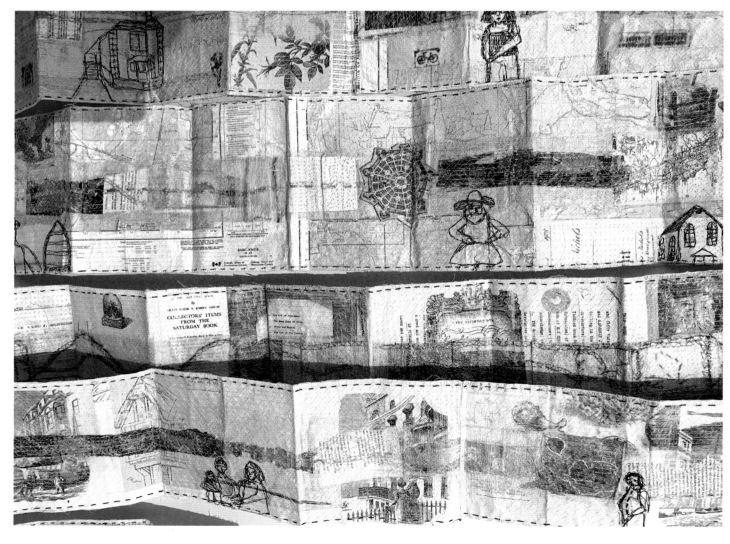

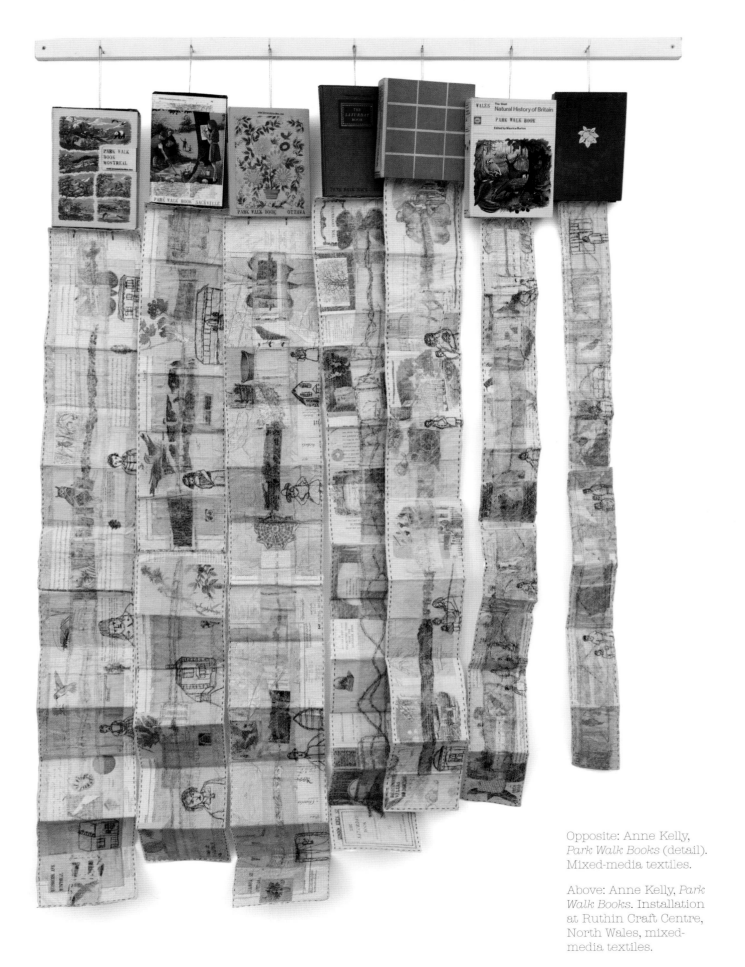

Opposite: Anne Kelly, *Park Walk Books* (detail). Mixed-media textiles.

Above: Anne Kelly, *Park Walk Books*. Installation at Ruthin Craft Centre, North Wales, mixed-media textiles.

Park Walk Books

I was honoured to be invited to exhibit at the renowned Ruthin Craft Centre in Wales in 2021. My solo exhibition, 'Well Travelled', was about travel and memory. It seemed fitting to create a series of folding book forms based on places in which I had lived. I used a map as a background with vintage ephemera and textiles combined with paper and tissue paper joined by stitch. I drew images of myself and family and friends, and free-motion stitched over the folding book forms.

When the pieces were finished, I put them into book cover 'boxes' that they could be stored in and hung from. The book boxes were created from book covers that were added to, with card sides and openings to hang the pieces from, and in the gallery they were hung together from a wooden rail.

Anne Kelly, *Park Walk Books* (detail), mixed-media textiles.

Making a Park Walk Book

First, decide on your theme – whether it be a place, a particular time or a specific memory. Hunt through your collections for ephemera and photos, either to use as reference to draw from or to use in your piece.

1 Use a piece cut from an old map or map brochure roughly 12 × 45cm (5 × 18in) in size as a background on which to lay out your pieces of ephemera. When you are happy with the arrangement, use a glue stick to place them.

2 Using about 65g (½ cup) of PVA glue, dilute it with water to make a 50/50 mixture. Use a wide brush to spread an even coat of this glue mixture over the whole piece.

3 Carefully cut a piece of good-quality white tissue paper to the same size as your map background and lay it on top. Brush with another coat of the diluted PVA mixture and leave to dry.

4 Once it is completely dry, iron your assembled piece between sheets of baking parchment or greaseproof paper.

5 Use a waterproof fine-line pen to draw your people over the assembled background piece, then stitch over them with free-motion embroidery or backstitch hand-stitching.

6 Embellish the background and add detail to your piece with hand- and machine-stitching.

7 Fold the piece using an iron to create the book.

Stay at Home

In this composite portrait, I combined individual images of my immediate family, stitched over a multi-layered and patched background. I used domestic textiles and family fabrics for the background. I wanted the faces of the family members to be superimposed over the textiles. I used the tracing method as described in Making a Self-Portrait on Cloth (pages 11–12) to draw the outlines and hand-stitched them using backstitch and perle cotton.

Opposite: Anne Kelly, *Stay at Home* (detail), mixed-media textile.

Below: Anne Kelly, *Stay at Home*, mixed-media textile, in studio.

Left: Anne Kelly, *Stay at Home*, mixed-media textile.

Opposite: Anne Kempton, *The Many Faces of Nalda Searles*, mixed-media sculpture.

'Ain't the Archies' Exhibition

Stay at Home was included as part of a wonderful group exhibition at the Timeless Textiles Gallery in Newcastle, in the Australian state of New South Wales. Twenty artists from around the world, who work with a range of fibre and textile techniques, were inspired by the Art Gallery of NSW's Archibald Prize (an Australian portraiture art prize for painting) to create portraits for the 'Ain't the Archies' exhibition. As the curator Anne Kempton explains:

> 'The Archibald Prize was first awarded in 1921 with a bequest from former editor of *The Bulletin*, J. F. Archibald. The competition has not only reflected Australian cultural history in artists' choice of subject matter, but also innovation and change in art styles and mediums.' 'For "Ain't the Archies", a diverse group of artists have created portraits either of themselves or of another fibre artist who has influenced them. As conceptually thrilling as it is aesthetically rich, "Ain't the Archies" features new works that reinterpret and reimagine portraiture. Artists of various ages and backgrounds, and hailing from different parts of Australia and the world, have created new works for this exhibition. Their works apply a range of textile-art techniques creating unique and inspired artworks.'

Anne Kempton: The Many Faces of Nalda Searles

Anne is the director of the Timeless Textiles Gallery and an artist in her own right. The piece that she included in the 'Ain't the Archies' exhibition tells its own fascinating story, as she explains:

'Nalda Searles is a highly regarded WA [Western Australia] fibre artist, who has spent decades working collaboratively with indigenous women in the bush. I am inspired by her love of interpretive mark-making; found objects and natural materials, including bush plant fibres; and her link to family history.'

'I have explored many techniques – felt-making, papier-mâché, drawing, abstractions, cement fondue, resin masks and screen-printing – in an attempt to present the many faces of Nalda Searles. The rusted tin frames encapsulate these faces, hopefully presenting one intriguing face … This artwork is a broad presentation of Nalda's materials and techniques, celebrating her unique contribution to fibre art – with a nod to her work by incorporating marks of red (stitching, kangaroo paws or glasses), handmade ink and dyes from the desert, and found objects.'

Sue Stone: Made in Grimsby

Sue is a British artist who has a long and distinguished history of portraiture in textile art, often telling stories about her family and personal history, as in her piece *Made in Grimsby*, as she explains:

'Between 1973 and 2002 I lived my life as a clothing designer. *Made in Grimsby* documents our small lifestyle clothing brand, "Anywear", which was a collaboration between myself and my husband, David Pitcher. We designed and manufactured womenswear from our Edwardian shop premises in Grimsby, North East Lincolnshire, in an area more associated with fish than clothing. In the early days, I designed "one-off" pieces and my husband designed the logos for prints on sweatshirts and T-shirts.'

Sue Stone, *Made in Grimsby*, mixed-media textile collage.

'There were many ups and downs during the lifespan of the business which provoked mixed emotions in the making of the pieces – the excitement of early choreographed fashion shows, the "one-off" designs, the opening of new shops and a foray into mail order (pre-internet); after this, a series of misfortunes led to the need to become more commercial and less creative. We decided to close the business in 2002 and I now have enough space to look back and be proud of my time as a designer, although I much prefer life as an artist.'

Right and below: Sue Stone, *Made in Grimsby* (details), mixed-media textile collage.

'*Made in Grimsby* (size 87.5 × 145cm) was made in response to an exhibition call-out from the 62 Group of Textile Artists, of which I am an exhibiting member. Graphic elements depict my ever-changing role as designer, pattern-drafter, cutter, sample-maker and finisher. They also show how our cloth was sourced. Anywear logos are from David's original designs for prints on sweats and tees. The Pitchers Anywear Fine Cloth design is from a wonderful pencil-crayon drawing by my father-in-law, Alf Pitcher. Clothing design shown in this piece is taken from my original drawings and some small design elements; the palm trees, for example, were applied fabrics. The portraits are of myself and my husband, sourced from original photos from 1975–2002.'

Emily Tull, *Woman with a Fish*, mixed-media textile.

Emily Tull: Woman with a Fish

Emily, an English textile artist based in Kent, is by her own admission 'obsessed with portraits'. I liked the referential nature of the work she created for the 'Ain't The Archies' exhibition at the Timeless Textiles Gallery, when she chose Sue Stone, whose pieces often feature a fish as a symbol of her heritage, as the subject for her textile portrait. She explains how she came to make this piece here:

'When I was asked to make a portrait of a fibre artist, I knew that I wanted to create a piece that was a combination of our two techniques. Although different visually, for me Sue Stone's style fitted perfectly alongside mine. The way she uses running stitch to capture facial features reminded me of my early outlining in brown. We also frame people – Sue with panels of stitching, and myself with fabric fragments. The tricky part was balancing the two and, of course, I wanted the fish reference. I found this lovely North Sea fish fabric which worked perfectly with the deep orange/reds of Sue's outfit and symbolized Grimsby. The fish are angled to counterbalance the portrait pose.'

Waiting Room Chair

This chair is a sculpture and receptacle for a series of drawings that I made during the pandemic, while on short breaks with my husband. It describes the time, story and emotions of waiting. During this period we were waiting to see family and friends abroad. Unable to travel, we were thinking about them and especially my father, who had recently died. He was a blood chemist and consequently the chair has a number of blood cell shapes, created by sewing old lace doilies onto printed backgrounds. I have also made block-printed fabric as a border, using cell shapes and colours. The dense and textural framing of the drawings create an almost veil-like quality, which again emphasizes separation.

Anne Kelly, *Waiting Room Chair*, mixed-media textile on wood and metal chair.

Left and above: Anne Kelly, studies for *Waiting Room Chair*, mixed media on paper.

Above and right: Anne Kelly, studies for *Waiting Room Chair*, ink on paper.

Seen here are the drawings that I used to make the panels that covered the chair. I used photocopies to free-motion stitch the outlines of the figures. These were then added to the decorative framing panels.

Making a Cover for an Upholstered Chair

To turn an upholstered chair or other piece of upholstered furniture into three-dimensional textile art, you will need sufficient calico or plain cotton fabric to cover your object twice (once as a base fabric and once as a pattern piece).

1 Cover your piece of furniture with a plain calico or cotton fabric, using a staple gun to staple it into place. Make sure it is taut and evenly applied.

2 Make a pattern for each element of your piece of furniture (in my case, chair back, inside front, seat) using brown or greaseproof paper, and allow for a 1cm (⅜in) seam allowance all around.

3 Pin your cut-out pattern pieces to calico or plain cotton fabric and cut them out.

4 Choose your pieces of stitched work, displaying them to advantage on the elements of your piece of furniture.

5 Pin your pieces to the covered object to see what they look like. When you are happy with the shapes and fit, stitch them to your pre-cut calico or plain cotton fabric pieces.

6 Staple and/or glue your embellished fabric pieces to the object to be covered, ensuring that you use the correct tools and a safe, stable space to work in.

Tilleke Schwarz: In Memoriam

Tilleke Schwarz is a renowned textile artist from the Netherlands who makes richly embellished, hand-stitched pieces. I was interested in the way that she combines text with portraiture. She stitches 'maps of modern life' that remind viewers of graffiti, as she describes:

> 'I include anything that moves, amazes or intrigues me. Daily life, mass media, traditional samplers and cats are major sources of inspiration. The result is a mixture of content – graphic quality and fooling around. The work can be understood as a kind of visual poetry.'

Tilleke Schwarz,
In Memoriam,
mixed-media textile.

Tilleke Schwarz,
In Memoriam (detail),
mixed-media textile.

'*In Memoriam* reminds me of the many relatives and friends who passed away in 1987/1988. In that year also a pet cat was killed by a car. The title is Latin and means "in remembrance". I first made the outline of the faces with textile paint and covered it with embroidery. The main embroidery technique is couching, a kind of writing and drawing with thread and needle. The two faces are actually a double portrait of one person: one in good health and the other (the white one) ill. The text refers to those who passed away in that period, so it is kind of a memory cloth, but it also questions if it is OK to make this kind of textile.'

Rosie James: Souvenir Badges

Rosie is a textile artist based in the south-east of England who has a distinctive stitch-sketch technique that she uses for her intricately observed drawings of people in various locations. I was drawn to these badge-style pieces, which were exhibited at the UK's Festival of Quilts in 2021, which she describes here:

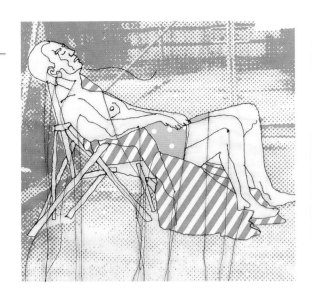

Rosie James, *Strood*, mixed-media textile collage.

Rosie James, *Aylesford*, mixed-media textile collage.

'There are four panels: Strood, Aylesford, Snodland, Larkfield. They are all places near to my home in a village in Kent. I became obsessed with the souvenir cloth patches collected by tourists, on holiday and travelling the world. They used to be sewn onto jackets and hats, in order to display all the exotic places to which they had travelled. It is interesting as to which towns and cities have cloth patches. I wanted to make some for those places to which no tourist goes – the suburbs, those unsung everyday places in which we spend a lot of time and don't even notice. My places are: the supermarket car park in Larkfield (which may have been a field of larks once!), the shops in Snodland, the roadworks in Strood, the back of the industrial estate in Aylesford.'

Rosie James,
Snodland, mixed-
media textile collage.

Rosie James,
Larkfield, mixed-
media textile collage.

FUR AND FEATHERS

Chapter 6

Pets and Animals

'Time spent with cats is never wasted.'

Sigmund Freud, Austrian neurologist and founder of psychoanalysis

Anne Kelly, *Animals Box*, mixed media.

Animal Imagery

Although cats are the only pets I have any experience of, I do understand how attached and connected people can be to their animals. It is enjoyable to make portraits and record memories of life with animals and pets. In this extra chapter, I am looking at how to create images of them with different techniques, formats and meanings. You will be able to find a way to incorporate animal imagery into your practice with some helpful examples and suggestions.

Anne Kelly, *Cat and Birds Home*, mixed-media textile.

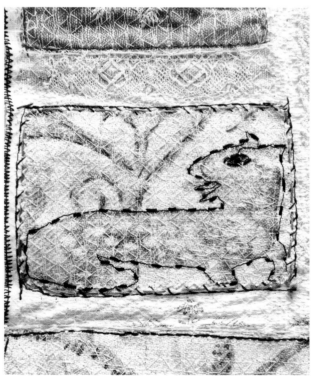

Cat Composition

I wanted to make a piece about my daughter and her kitten, taken from an old photo. I used a piece of canvas as a background and drew a picture of her from the photo, adding the objects around her to become part of the picture. I outlined the main elements with a dark blue or black outline, and then used machine embroidery, free-motion and some straight stitching to fill in the main objects. When I was finished, I mounted the canvas on a heavier piece of blanket cloth.

Janine Heschl: Wildlife Inspirations

Janine is a self-taught textile wildlife artist based in Austria. I was drawn to two aspects of her work: her studies of animal eyes and her endangered bird series. Describing her practice, she says:

'The wild animal kingdom is my greatest source of inspiration. I am fascinated by the patterns, designs, colours, eyes, textures … I look at animal photography and immediately zoom into the details and am left breathless with what reveals itself before my eyes. This is when my passion kicks in and I feel the urge to recreate what I just witnessed in a textile portrait.'

'All my portraits start out with a good couple of hours of scanning through websites with wildlife reference photos. I don't always go looking for a certain subject or pose; I just wait for that tingle at the back of my neck when looking at the photos, because that tells me that I have found what I was looking for. I let the animals find me, rather than the other way around. The next step is to choose the size of the portrait and to create a sketch of the subject on my background fabric with a pencil. This is followed by the process of creating a detailed fabric collage using mainly batik fabric snippets on top of that sketch, which will serve as my navigational map.'

'My entire embroidery process is based on layering thread to create realism. This is why I choose to work with the thinnest thread available for most of my portraits, to avoid thread bulk or puckering, and the latter is minimized by the use of a wooden hoop for the stability and tension of the fabric during stitching. I always start out with the eyes, as they are the most difficult as well as revealing part of the portrait. They set the emotion and the mood for the entire piece, so I usually spend about two hours on each eye to really get them right and to create expression. Once those are done, I fan out with my embroidering process and work my way towards the edges. I tend to lay down the direction of the hairs or feathers in my very first layer and build up upon that. It takes some time to understand your subject, to really study the details, the colours and the composition, and then translate it into thread.'

Janine Heschl, *Great Horned Owl Forest Spirit*, embroidery on cloth.

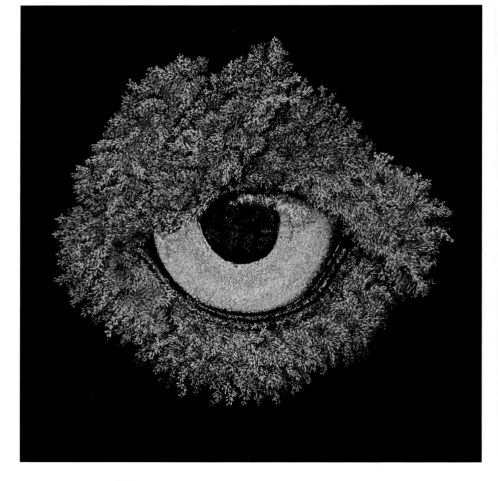

Janine's series of work, 'Fade of Songs', about the disappearance of songbirds, echoes my own artwork series, 'Sparrow Stories', produced in collaboration with the RSPB, so I was interested to discover more about her process. She worked with multiple media, as she describes here:

'Using Inktense blocks and pencils, I have drawn a faint sketch of the subject on a vintage cotton fabric and then applied thread with my sewing machine in free-motion. I deliberately embroidered the birds' top halves in full, carefully letting their feathers thin out at their bellies and tails. I wanted to create a fading effect, emphasizing and drawing attention to the disappearance of our songbirds in Europe. The colour splashes on the background fabric should also remind us of the vulnerability of our wildlife and how we must take responsibility for action, before it "dissolves" right before our own eyes.'

British Textile Biennial

I was delighted to be a part of the British Textile Biennial 2021. My piece, *Robin*, was just one of over a hundred 15cm (6in) hoop embroideries on display in Blackburn Cathedral in the 'Stitch Your Story' group exhibition, organized by Mr X Stitch (Jamie Chalmers), who describes the event as follows:

'The "Stitch Your Story" installation in Blackburn Cathedral was an international collection of 118 hand embroideries from 19 countries that express people's stories of movement and place. It was a really wonderful exhibition filled with moving stories (pun intended) as well as sublime stitching, and the installation as a whole was a gentle collection of personal narratives that encourage you to spend time in conversation with the creators. Whenever you launch a collaborative art project like 'Stitch Your Story', there's no way of knowing what the end result will be, which can prove challenging from a project management standpoint, and is also somewhat nerve-wracking to begin with. However, if I've learned anything from projects like this, it's that if you give stitchers a good reason to make something, they will rise to the occasion. And that was precisely what happened this time!'

Above: Anne Kelly, *Robin*, mixed media on textile with wooden hoop.

Left: Anne Kelly, 'Bird Postcards', mixed-media textile collage.

As you can see from my 'Bird Postcards' series, I also enjoy working on a smaller scale and these were made for exhibition recently. Postcards are a good way to create small artworks and to experiment with technique and collage. There are more examples of bird postcards a little later in this chapter from two artists who have made wonderful contributions to the genre.

Making a Bird Portrait

This has been an extremely popular workshop and I enjoy delivering it in many different settings, including as a Zoom workshop during the pandemic.

Above: Anne Kelly, *Quail* (detail), mixed-media textile with wooden hoop.

Left: Anne Kelly, *Quail*, mixed-media textile with wooden hoop.

1 Select a good, clear bird image to work from and use tracing paper to trace it onto your background fabric, using a neutral or embroidered strong cotton, canvas or linen fabric no larger than A4 in size. Outline the image firmly with a pencil or fine-line pen.

2 Working from your fabric collections, choose small pieces of fabric to fill in the bird within the outline, adding the wings and legs/feet, beak and eye in that order.

3 Use a glue stick to lightly glue the pieces onto the background and tack them in place using stab stitches and a neutral thread. Then you can begin to embroider details, like feathers, with coloured embroidery cotton.

4 Approach the background in the same way – it can be as simple or complex as you wish.

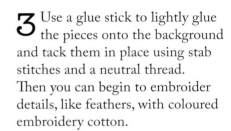

Above left: Anne Kelly, *Wood Pigeon*, mixed-media textile with wooden hoop.

Left: Wendy Shaw, bird collage from Hope & Elvis workshop.

Making an Animal Textile Sculpture

I have found that an uncomplicated way to make an animal sculpture is to cover a papier-mâché form with fabric pieces. These forms are readily available at craft shops or online. First, choose your animal – I chose a horse.

1 Selecting a lightweight fabric to give your piece a good base colour, use a glue stick to cover the entire papier-mâché form with it.

2 Working from your fabric collections in your chosen range of colours and textures, find pieces of fabric – embroidered or quilted, and some plain – that will accentuate the shape of your animal: back, legs, head, etc.

3 Working from largest to smallest and using a glue gun for bigger pieces, glue the largest pieces on first.

4 If you want to include stitched details, like the 'saddle' on my horse, stitch them separately and add them at the end of the process.

Karen Nicol: Postcard Pieces

Karen is a renowned embroidery and mixed-media textile artist with many years of experience, working in galleries, fashion and interiors with a London-based design and production studio established for over 25 years. She specializes in Irish, Cornelly and hand embroidery. I love these 'postcard pieces', where she combines collages of people with birds.

Above: Karen Nicol, *Miles to Go Before I Sleep*, mixed-media textile collage.

Above: Karen Nicol, *Delicious Eavesdropping*, mixed-media textile collage.

Below: Karen Nicol, *Ready for Takeoff*, mixed-media textile collage.

Kathryn Harmer Fox: Postcard Series

I met Kathryn while tutoring in Australia and New Zealand. Her exuberant and confident teaching style is echoed in her beautifully detailed and colourful work, mainly of animals from her native South Africa. She sells these printed textiles as patterns for others to stitch.

Above: Kathryn Harmer Fox, *Barn Owl*, printed textile from original.

Left: Kathryn Harmer Fox, *Secretary Bird*, printed textile from original.

Kathryn Harmer Fox, printed owl postcards on cloth.

Rabbit Sewing Basket and Owl Case

Here I used the same technique as described in Making a Bird Portrait (see pages 113–114), featured a little later in this chapter, to create the top of my rabbit sewing basket. I source pre-loved sewing baskets from charity shops and enjoy re-covering them.

Above: Anne Kelly, *Owl Case*, mixed-media textile on cardboard case.

Left: Anne Kelly, *Owl Case* (top view), mixed-media textile on cardboard case.

Students love to create objects and I have made two prototypes for workshops using pet portraits. The owl was a design for a possible embroidery template which became a cover for a small suitcase. I love repurposing items like this.

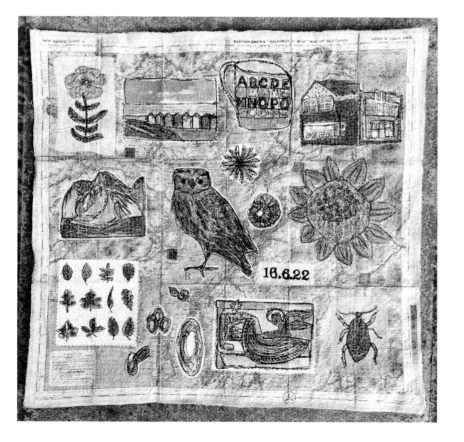

I also enjoy creating commissions for special occasions and I used the owl theme again in this piece for a recent big birthday celebration.

Conclusion

'If people say, "You can't do that", you can be sure I will do my utmost to do it.'

Cornelia Parker, British contemporary artist

People and animals are probably the most difficult type of subject matter to tackle when making textile pieces. Although textile portraiture can be very challenging, it is so worthwhile when you are able to explore it. All aspects of life should be 'on the table' when it comes to making work and developing a theme. Drawing is important when designing this type of work, and I hope that the examples in this book will encourage you to try your own.

I am very fortunate in my tutoring career to share accomplishments with students when they have been working on portraiture as a theme. It is very rewarding to see their achievements develop into works in cloth. I enjoy watching their confidence progress as they get to grips with a new approach to making.

I have been making portraiture-themed work myself and completing some larger-scale pieces as part of recent major exhibitions. I've learnt a lot about protest movements and combining meaning with image in this new textile journey. Although nostalgia is comforting and a good starting point for figurative imagery, I like to look to the future and how new generations will approach this most evocative of themes.

Anne Kelly's studio wall.

Featured Artists and Contributors

Louise Asher	www.instagram.com/lou_ash_art	Melanie Bowles	www.stitch-school.com
Claire A. Baker	www.claireabaker.co.uk	Andrea Cryer	www.andreacryer.co.uk
Darren Ball	www.darrenballtextileartist.com	Jenni Dutton	www.jennidutton.com
Anuradha Bhaumick	www.anuradhabhaumick.com	Johanna Flanagan	www.thepalerook.com
Neil Bottle	www.neilbottle.co.uk	James Fox	www.jamesfoxtextileartist.co.uk

Caren Garfen www.carengarfen.com
Emily Jo Gibbs www.emilyjogibbs.co.uk
Megan Ivy Griffiths www.meganivygriffiths.co.uk
Kathryn Harmer-Fox www.artblr.com/kathrynharmerfox/en
Jenny Hart www.jennyhartstudio.com

Janine Heschl www.textilewildlifeart.com
Catherine Hill www.arnolds-attic.co.uk/tag/catherine-hill-textile-artist
Faith Humphrey Hill www.dartily.com
Michelle Holmes www.archangelstudio.co.uk/michelle-holmes
Rosie James www.rosiejamestextileartist.wordpress.com/about
Anne Kempton www.timelesstextiles.com.au/artist/anne-kempton-3
Summer Kiser www.instagram.com/summerkiser
Marna Lunt bio.site/marnaluntartist
Joetta Maue www.joettamaue.com
David Morrish www.kingfly.co.uk
Karen Nicol www.karennicol.com
Frances Palgrave www.mystitchart.jimdofree.com
Mary Tooley Parker www.marytooleyparker.com
Lynne and
 Michael Roche www.roche-dolls.co.uk
Tilleke Schwarz www.tillekeschwarz.com
Diana Springall www.dianaspringallcollection.co.uk
Sue Stone www.womanwithafish.com
Maria Thomas www.mariathomastextiles.co.uk
Kasia Tons www.kasiarosetons.com
Emily Tull www.emilytull.co.uk
Willemien de Villiers www.willemiendevilliers.co.za
Sally Welchman www.moggshop.com
Suzy Wright www.orangethread.co.uk
Sarah Young www.sarah-young.co.uk
Melissa Zexter www.melissazexter.com

Anne Kelly's studio.

For Investigation

The Amelia Scott
www.theamelia.co.uk

Bishopsgate Institute
www.bishopsgate.org.uk

Crafts Council
www.craftscouncil.org.uk

Embroiderers' Guild
www.embroiderersguild.com

Embroidery magazine
www.embroiderymagazine.co.uk

European Textile Network
www.etn-net.org

Glasgow Women's Library
www.womenslibrary.org.uk

The Harley Gallery
www.harleygallery.co.uk

National Portrait Gallery
www.npg.org.uk

Pour l'Amour du Fil
www.pourlamourdufil.com

The Quilters' Guild
www.quiltersguild.org.uk

Ruthin Craft Centre
www.ruthincraftcentre.org.uk

Society for Embroidered Work
www.societyforembroideredwork.com

Society of Designer Craftsmen
societyofdesignercraftsmen.org.uk

Textile Society of America
www.textilesocietyofamerica.org

Timeless Textiles
www.timelesstextiles.com.au

The Women's Library LSE
www.lse.ac.uk/library/collection-highlights/the-womens-library

Anne Kelly, drawing on cloth and sketchbook portraits, mixed media.

Anne Kelly, 'Folding Books', mixed media.

Further Reading

Fabric of a Nation: American Quilt Stories, MFA Publications, 2021

Campbell-Harding, Valerie, *Faces and Figures in Embroidery*, Batsford Books, 1979

Holmes, Cas and Kelly, Anne, *Connected Cloth*, Batsford Books, 2013

James, Rosie, *Stitch Draw: Design and Techniques for Figurative Stitching*, Batsford Books, 2018

Kelly, Anne, *Textile Folk Art*, Batsford Books, 2018

Kelly, Anne, *Textile Nature*, Batsford Books, 2016

Kelly, Anne, *Textile Travels*, Batsford Books, 2020

Pill, Katherine and Watt, Melinda, *Gio Swaby*, Rizzoli International Publications, 2022

Singer, Ruth, *Criminal Quilts,* Independent Publishing Network, 2020

Warren, Erica, *Bisa Butler: Portraits*, Yale University Press, 2020

Suppliers

UK

Bernina UK
91 Goswell Road
London EC1V 7EX
Tel: 020 7549 7849
www.bernina.co.uk

Jackson's Art Supplies
1 Farleigh Place
London N16 7SX
Tel: 020 7254 0077
www.jacksonsart.com

Loop London
15 Camden Passage
London N1 8EA
Tel: 020 7288 1160
loopknitting.com

Seawhite
Avalon Court
Star Road Trading Estate
Partridge Green
Horsham RH13 8RY
01403 711633
www.seawhite.co.uk

Shepherds Art Supplies
30 Gillingham Street
London SW1V 1HU
020 7233 9999
store.bookbinding.co.uk/store/

George Weil
Old Portsmouth Road
Peasmarsh
Guildford GU3 1LZ
01483 565800
www.georgeweil.com

Art Textile Courses

UK

Bath Textile Summer School
www.bathtextilesummerschool.co.uk

Cowslip Workshops
www.cowslipworkshops.co.uk

Hope & Elvis
www.hopeandelvis.com

West Dean College of Arts &
Conservation
www.westdean.org.uk

USA and Canada

French General
www.frenchgeneral.com/collections/
workshops

Maiwa School of Textiles
maiwa.teachable.com

Australia and New Zealand

Fibre Arts Take Two
www.fibreartstaketwo.com

Grampians Texture
www.grampianarts.com.au

Textile Fest
www.textilefest.com.au

Creative Fibre
www.creativefibre.org.nz

Above: Portrait photo
of Anne Kelly hand-
stitching.

Opposite: Anne Kelly,
Young Visitors (detail),
mixed-media textile.

Acknowledgements

My thanks to the artists, makers and contributors named in the text. Their details are in Featured Artists and Contributors on pages 112–123.

Special thanks to my editors Tina Persaud and Nicola Newman at Batsford Books.

For Jesse, his parents and grandparents, aunts and uncles, cousins and friends.

Photo Credits

Book photography: Rachel Whiting
Additional Anne Kelly photos:
Alun Callender, Dewi Tannatt Lloyd
Craig McCann-McMillan (Claire A. Baker)
Tas Kyrianou (Emily Jo Gibbs)
Lal Johnson (Emily Jo Gibbs)

Index

animal textile sculpture 115
Asher, Louise 63

bag 42, 43
Baker, Claire A. 37
Ball, Darren 73
Bhaumick, Anuradha 23
birds 110, 111, 112, 114, 118, 119
Bishopsgate Institute 36
Bottle, Neil 85
Bourgeois, Louise 50, 51
Bowles, Melanie 59
British Textile Biennial 112

cat composition 109
Co-operative Women's Guild 36
Cryer, Andrea 19

de Villiers, Willemien 39
Dickinson, Emily 60, 61
doll collections 64–65
doll-making 50, 51, 55–57
Dutton, Jenni 74

Embroiderers' Guild 40

Flanagan, Johanna 52
Fox, James 38
French General 80

Garfen, Caren 32
Gibbs, Emily-Jo 18
Griffiths, Megan Ivy 54

Hand & Lock 40
Harmer-Fox, Kathryn 117
Hart, Jenny 46
Heschl, Janine 110, 111
Hill, Catherine 20
Hill, Faith Humphrey 22
holidays 14, 15
Holmes, Michelle 44

James, Rosie 104, 105

Kempton, Anne 95
Kiser, Summer 84
Knitting and Stitching Show 20, 21

Lambert, Mariam 80
Lunt, Marna 4, 46

Maue, Joetta 13
Morrish, David 40

Nicol, Karen 116

owl case 118

Palgrave, Frances 26
Park Walk Books 90, 91
Parker, Mary Tooley 33
photographs, using 71, 75, 77

rabbit sewing basket 119
Roche, Lynne and Michael 62
Ruthin Craft Centre 30, 31, 88, 89, 90, 91

Schwarz, Tilleke 102, 103
Scott, Amelia 34, 35
self-portraits 10–12
Springall, Diana 21
Stone, Sue 96, 97

Thomas, Maria 82
Timeless Textiles Gallery 24–27, 42, 43
Tons, Kasia 53
Tull, Emily 98

Wright, Suzy 27

Young, Sarah 58

Zexter, Melissa 83